The Way of Prayer

The Way of Prayer

By
PETER AINSLIE

WILDSIDE PRESS

Contents

CONTENTS

Foreword

RECENTLY, I took a year's leave of absence from my ministry in Baltimore in order to visit as many universities and colleges in the United States as that time would permit, speaking on the adjustment of international and interracial disputes by courts of justice, rather than by physical force, and the necessity of a united Christendom for the accomplishment of these things. My tour extended as far west as California and I delivered in all more than two hundred addresses. In many instances I met in conference student groups for the discussion of spiritual life. Out of these conferences I have prepared this little book in an attempt both to answer, and to give direction to, some of the inquiries.

This book emphasizes prayer in individual experience. One need not be discouraged because he cannot find adjustment at once in this greater fellowship. It is a thing of growth. One gradually goes beyond his community, his communion, his nation, and his race in most things. Why should he not do so in spiritual experience until he reaches the secret sources of the Kingdom of God and himself becomes an echo of the love of God?

We ourselves are part of the tides of discouragement, anxiety, unreality, and selfishness. These can only be met by lives of intercession and thanksgiving. Both persons and conditions look better after we have prayed for them. The processes for the triumph of righteousness are already in permanent action. We discover that, as Goethe so well says: "Everything transitory is parable." The outward and visible are temporary and are themselves a succession of parables, from which we are to learn the lessons of reality, as long ago Christ gave his parables to illustrate living truths. God's goodness is stronger than man's sin. The established habit of intercession and thanksgiving is the remedy for the unrest in human experience.

I have purposely quoted from many books, giving the author, the title, and the publisher, as an aid for further study of this great subject, whose frontiers have been barely touched by this little volume.

Baltimore, Md.

HAVE YOU A CASTLE?

Everybody should have a castle, built so high upon the mountain peaks of the mind that the meaner self cannot climb to its heights, and so fortified that the approaches are guarded by white winged messengers from above.

There run occasionally for rest, out of the toil and vexations of life, as well as for a calm look upon the entangled problems of the world, that you may find where to lose yourself for the good of others.

If you have not built such a castle, build it at once. Find the highest mountain in your mind—one of those that reaches highest into the blue vault of thought—and fortify as you build.

If your place in life lies mostly with those minds that are low and marshy, whence arises the malaria of discontent, lust, suspicion, and unlove, build your castle quickly and so protect your mountain passes that approaches to it will be impossible except to yourself and the angels that minister there.

Then you will be patient in the midst of the strife of the lower souls, you will do good to those who have wronged you, and your pity for all shall lie like a beam of light upon every face into which you shall look. The needs of every one shall come before you like the pathetic cry of the helpless infant, and your castle life shall make you a brother to all mankind.

THE PRIMACY OF PRAYER

THE getting together of God and ourselves is the great ideal of human life. It is the fundamental basis of all good. It is God's method of changing us from what we are to what we ought to be. Every prayer is an idea of God seeking expression in the human soul to make us want what God wants us to be. The chief activities of prayer lie in personal communion with God and intercession for others.

IN SECRET—" Pray to thy Father who is in secret " (Matt. 6:6). It is God's invitation to shut the door with Him and us alone. There our true life lives. Our sin, our guilt, and our grief must be all uncovered before Him. Those things that harass and hurt and soil the soul must be looked upon by Him and us alone. Letting out our heart's need to God is true prayer. The uncovering of our soul's sickness to our " Father who is in secret " is to put the life of health into our souls. In that mystical chamber of solitude we learn the meaning of his Fatherhood and linger like children about the object of our love.

INTERCESSION—" Pray one for another " (Jas. 5:16). The most sacred exercise in which we can engage is to take time in beseeching God to pardon the transgressions of others, to comfort them with his Holy Spirit, and to give them eternal life. Intercessory prayer is committed to all Christians. It is the rule of Christian fellowship, including all and every part of the whole Church. The Apostle Paul made perpetual intercession for his fellow Christians. Mutual prayer for one another was the bond of unity and concord in the early Church. It is by praying for those who have hurt us and those who hate us that we learn to forgive them. It is the cure for personal enmities, for littleness of soul, and for divisions in the Church. There is no exercise in human experience which will bring more inward peace, a more universal fellowship, and make more permanent the Kingdom of God in the souls of men than praying one for another.

Prayer is the gateway to life; it is the pulse of the soul; and in its exercise we establish transactions between the two great realities—God and ourselves.

[9]

CALL TO PRAYER

O come, let us worship and bow down.

Know ye that the Lord He is God: it is He that hath made us, and not we ourselves; we are his people, and the sheep of his pasture.

Enter into his gates with thanksgiving, and into his courts with praise; be thankful unto Him, and bless his name.

—Psa. 95: 6; 100: 3, 4.

Seeing then that we have a great high priest, that is passed into the heavens, Jesus the Son of God, let us hold fast our profession. For we have not a high priest which cannot be touched with the feeling of our infirmities; but was in all points tempted like as we are, yet without sin. Let us, therefore, come boldly unto the throne of grace, that we may obtain mercy, and find grace to help in time of need.

—Heb. 4: 14-16.

Be careful for nothing; but in every thing by prayer and supplication with thanksgiving let your requests be made known unto God.

—Phil. 4: 6.

Do not pray by idle rote like pagans, for they suppose they will be heard the more they say; you must not copy them; your Father knows your needs before you ask Him.

—Matt. 6: 7, 8 (Moffatt).

OUR BLESSED LORD hath recommended his love to us, as the pattern and example of our love to one another. As, therefore, He is continually making intercession for us all, so ought we to intercede and pray for one another.

—WILLIAM LAW. *A Serious Call.*

[10]

CALL TO PRAYER

MEDITATION:

On our need of worship.

On our need of a deeper experimental knowledge of God.

On our need of a growing faith and an abounding love.

On our need of patience with one another until we shall see in all souls the mirror of God.

THANKSGIVING:

For God's gift to the world of his only begotten Son, Jesus Christ, our Lord and Saviour.

For the gift of the Holy Spirit, by whom we are sealed unto the day of redemption.

For the gift of the Church, which is held under the purchase of Jesus Christ.

For the gift of the Bible, by which we come to know Christ in the days of his flesh, and the interpretation of those days by those nearest to Him.

For the task in facing a world in process of redemption.

PENITENCE:

For our personal sins.

For thinking and speaking unkindly of others and our indifference to the needs of others.

For our failure to exercise our souls in intercessory prayer for the whole Church of God.

For our pride in theological interpretations and our aloofness in our relations with other Christians.

PETITION:

For the coming of the Kingdom of God.

For blessing upon the whole Church.

For practical application of the principles of Christian brotherhood in all human relations—religious, social, industrial, interracial, and international.

For the leadership of the Holy Spirit.

DAY BY DAY—PRAYER FOR DAILY CLAIMS

The gates of heaven are lightly locked.
—C. K. CHESTERTON. *The Ballad of the White Horse.*

———

Rejoice evermore. Pray without ceasing. In every thing give thanks: for this is the will of God in Christ Jesus concerning you.

—1 Thess. 5: 16–18.

———

For God is my witness, whom I serve with my spirit in the Gospel of his Son, that without ceasing I make mention of you always in my prayers.

—Rom. 1: 9.

———

God forbid that I should sin against the Lord in ceasing to pray for you.

—1 Sam. 12: 23.

———

What things soever ye desire, when ye pray, believe that ye receive them, and ye shall have them. And when ye stand praying, forgive, if ye have aught against any: that your Father also which is in heaven may forgive you your trespasses.

—Mark 11:24, 25.

———

You do ask and you do not get it, because you ask with the wicked intention of spending it on your pleasures.

—Jas. 4: 3 (Moffatt).

———

If I regard iniquity in my heart, the Lord will not hear me: But verily God hath heard me; He hath attended to the voice of my prayer. Blessed be God, which hath not turned away my prayer, nor his mercy from me.

—Psa. 66:18–20.

[12]

DAY BY DAY—PRAYER FOR DAILY CLAIMS

FOR THE KINGDOM OF GOD:
> For the promise of the Kingdom.
> For the reality of the Kingdom.
> For the righteousness, peace, and joy of the Kingdom.
> For the hastening of the Kingdom.

FOR THE RULE OF THE HOLY SPIRIT:
> For the indwelling of the Spirit.
> For the intercession of the Spirit.
> For penitence for grief to the Spirit.
> For the witness of the Spirit.

FOR PERSONAL RELATIONSHIPS:
> For the family, near relatives, and dear friends.
> For wisdom and strength for the day's task.
> For food and shelter.
> For those whom we shall meet or have met in the day.

———

> Show me thy ways, O Lord;
> Teach me thy paths.
> Lead me in thy truth, and teach me;
> For Thou art the God of my salvation;
> On Thee do I wait all the day. Amen.
> > —*Psa. 25: 4, 5.*

———

ALMIGHTY FATHER, in whom we live and move and have our being; Lord of life and Shepherd of all! Hear us, and suffer not our hearts to fail us, but give us day by day such grace that we may help to bring thy Kingdom. Make our souls to be lamps of thine, lighted by Thee and kept burning by Thee, until the darkness of sin shall be wiped out, and the light of a living faith be in the hearts of all for whom we pray—ourselves and all who turn their faces toward Thee in prayer; through Jesus Christ our Lord. Amen.

[13]

Sunday

PRAYER FOR THE WHOLE CHURCH

Praying always with all prayer and supplication in the Spirit, and watching thereunto with all perseverance and supplication for all saints.

—Eph. 6: 18.

———

And other sheep I have, which are not of this fold: them also I must bring, and they shall hear my voice; and there shall be one fold, and one shepherd.

—John 10: 16.

———

Holy Father, keep through thine own name those whom Thou hast given Me, that they may be one, as We are. . . . Neither pray I for these alone, but for them also which shall believe on Me through their word; that they all may be one; as Thou, Father, art in Me, and I in Thee, that they also may be one in Us: that the world may believe that Thou hast sent Me.

—John 17: 11, 20, 21.

———

If we confess our sins, He is faithful and just to forgive us our sins, and to cleanse us from all unrighteousness. If we say that we have not sinned, we make Him a liar, and his word is not in us.

—I John 1:9, 10.

———

This cup is the new testament in my blood: this do ye, as oft as ye drink it, in remembrance of Me. For as often as ye eat this bread, and drink this cup, ye do show the Lord's death till He come.

—I Cor. 11: 25, 26.

———

By this shall all men know that ye are my disciples, if ye have love one to another.

—John 13: 35.

Sunday
PRAYER FOR THE WHOLE CHURCH

For Its Unity:
> For friendly attitudes between all Christians—Eastern Orthodox, Roman Catholics, Anglicans, Protestants, and all other Christians.
>
> For penitence among all Christians because of the universal schism.
>
> For rediscovery by all Christians of truth and love.
>
> For blessing upon all Christian unity movements and ventures toward unity.

For Its Servants:
> For ministers, authors, editors, artists, and all who seek to interpret God by voice, or pen, or brush.
>
> For church officials—those in high places, and those in local churches.
>
> For the faithful, the indifferent, and the new converts.
>
> For church workers in general, including the choir and friendly visitors.

For Its Services:
> For the public worship and the ordinances.
>
> For the evidences of spiritual growth in the lives of believers.
>
> For the Sunday-school, Christian Endeavour societies, guilds, etc.
>
> For the Young Men's Christian Associations, Young Women's Christian Associations, Bible societies, orphanages, homes for the aged, incurables, etc.

———

As the hart panteth after the water brooks,
So panteth my soul after Thee, O God. Amen.
                                        —*Psa. 42: 1.*

———

Most Merciful God and Father, we thank Thee that, in spite of our divisions, Thou hast loved us, and art ever seeking to make thyself known to us, that we may love each other fervently with pure minds and true hearts, thereby proving ourselves to be disciples of the Lord Jesus. Guide us that our footsteps may honour Thee, whose we are and whom we serve. Amen.

[15]

Monday

PRAYER FOR THOSE IN SORROW AND SICKNESS

Fear thou not; for I am with thee; be not dismayed; for I am thy God: I will strengthen thee; yea, I will help thee; yea, I will uphold thee with the right hand of my righteousness.

—Isa. 41: 10.

———

Thus also the Spirit helps us in our weakness. For we do not know what to pray for as we ought, but the Spirit itself intercedes for us with sighs beyond words. And He who searches hearts knows what is the mind of the Spirit, because He intercedes for the holy according to the will of God. We know that all things work together for good to those who love God, to those who are called according to his purpose.

—Rom. 8: 26–28 (Riverside).

———

Is any among you afflicted? let him pray. . . . Is any sick among you? let him call for the elders of the Church; and let them pray over him, anointing him with oil in the name of the Lord: And the prayer of faith shall save the sick, and the Lord shall raise him up; and if he have committed sins, they shall be forgiven him. Confess your faults one to another, and pray one for another, that ye may be healed. The effectual fervent prayer of a righteous man availeth much.

—Jas. 5: 13–16.

———

You might almost as well try to cure disease by prayer without treatment, as to try to cure it by treatment without prayer. You must use both.
—Sir Oliver Lodge.

Monday

PRAYER FOR THOSE IN SORROW AND SICKNESS

For Those in Sorrow:
  For persons who have had personal loss.
  For persons who have had great calamity.
  For persons who have suffered mistreatment and per-
    secution.
  For the poor, the aged, and the lonely.

For Those in Sickness:
  For persons who have been cured.
  For persons with general sickness.
  For persons with incurable diseases, including the
    blind, the deaf, the dumb, the insane, etc.
  For persons who are nearing the end of the earthly life.

For Helpers:
  For spiritual visitors to those in sorrow and sickness.
  For physicians, surgeons, and nurses.
  For hospitals and sanitariums.
  For friends and benefactors to the sick and sorrowing.

———

Be merciful unto me, O God, be merciful unto me;
For my soul trusteth in Thee:
Yea, in the shadow of thy wings will I make my refuge,
Until these calamities be overpast.   Amen.

—Psa. 57: 1.

———

O Lord, Thou art the shadow of a great rock in a weary
land. Sorrow and sickness are abundant around us. Thou
art our refuge. Comfort those in sorrow, heal the sick, o'r,
if not thy will to heal, make thy grace sufficient for them
while they live, and give them the abundance of thy mercy
when Thou takest them into thy rest. Bless all those who
help to alleviate the pain of body and mind. Do for us
what we have not the courage to do for ourselves, and may
we be wholly thine in that way that will be most for thy
glory; through Jesus Christ our Lord. Amen.

[17]

Tuesday

PRAYER FOR THE SOCIAL AWAKENING

The rich and poor meet together: the Lord is the maker of them all.

—Prov. 22: 2.

———

And when ye spread forth your hands, I will hide mine eyes from you: yea, when ye make many prayers, I will not hear: your hands are full of blood. Wash you, make you clean; put away the evil of your doings from before mine eyes; cease to do evil; learn to do well; seek judgment, relieve the oppressed, judge the fatherless, plead for the widow.

—Isa. 1: 15–17.

———

Every man according as he purposeth in his heart, so let him give; not grudgingly, or of necessity; for God loveth a cheerful giver.

—2 Cor. 9: 7.

———

The Spirit of the Lord is upon Me, because He hath anointed Me to preach the Gospel to the poor; He hath sent Me to heal the broken-hearted, to preach deliverance to the captives, and recovering of sight to the blind, to set at liberty them that are bruised, to preach the acceptable year of the Lord.

—Luke 4: 18, 19.

———

What doth the Lord require of thee, but to do justly, and to love mercy, and to walk humbly with thy God?

—Micah 6: 8.

Tuesday

PRAYER FOR THE SOCIAL AWAKENING

FOR SOCIAL ADJUSTMENT:

For the rebirth of the individual soul, and the redis-
covery of personality.

For the establishment of Christian democracy.

For prisoners and all penal institutions.

For the social brotherhood of the world and the aboli-
tion of war.

FOR EMPLOYER AND EMPLOYEE:

For better understanding and appreciation.

For the establishment of coöperative methods.

For definite alliances for the good of each.

For a code of honour that will give equal dignity to
the holder of wealth and the holder of labour.

FOR THE HOME LIFE:

For the maintenance of the reality of religion in the
home, especially prayers for fathers and mothers,
children and servants.

For the sanctification of marriage.

For the right of a child to have a chance, and prayer
for all children.

For the home's common debt to the community.

Create in me a clean heart, O God;
And renew a right spirit within me.
Cast me not away from thy presence;
And take not thy Holy Spirit from me. Amen.
—*Psa. 51: 10, 11.*

O HOLY FATHER, have mercy upon us, and hasten the day
when all men shall discover that we are brothers in factory,
shop, store, field, mine, government, and wherever else men
are. Grant that men shall hold money lightly and shall
cease to defraud one another, and that the stewardship of
Divine love be held so sacredly that we shall be restless
and ill at ease because of the world's discontent and the
coldness of unbrotherly attitudes; through Jesus Christ to
whom be glory for ever. Amen.

[19]

Wednesday

PRAYER FOR WORLD-WIDE EVANGELIZATION

And Jesus came to them and spake unto them, saying, All authority hath been given unto Me in heaven and on earth. Go ye, therefore, and make disciples of all the nations, baptizing them into the name of the Father and of the Son and of the Holy Spirit: teaching them to observe all things whatsoever I commanded you: and lo, I am with you always, even unto the end of the world.

—*Matt. 28: 18–20 (R. V.).*

The harvest truly is great, but the labourers are few: pray ye, therefore, the Lord of the harvest, that He would send forth labourers into his harvest.

—*Luke 10: 2.*

Ask of Me, and I will give thee the nations for thine inheritance, and the uttermost parts of the earth for thy possession.

—*Psa. 2: 8 (R. V.).*

A Christian who is not really in heart and will a missionary is not a Christian at all. Missionary effort is not a specialty of a few Christians, though, like every other part of Christian life, it has its special organs. It is an essential, never to be forgotten, part of all true Christian living, and thinking, and praying. . . . Come then, O breath of the Divine Spirit and breathe upon the dead bones of the Christian churches that forget that they are evangelists of the nations, that they may live and stand upon their feet, an exceeding great army, an army with banners.

—CHARLES GORE. *Epistle to the Ephesians.*

Wednesday

PRAYER FOR WORLD-WIDE EVANGELIZATION

FOR MISSIONARY ACTIVITIES:

For all missionaries in all lands.

For all converts to Christ through missionary labours.

For all boards and churches that support missionary work, including local societies.

For more labourers in the harvest, including the Student Volunteers, etc.

FOR THE FOREIGN FIELD:

For larger freedom in coöperation among Christians on the foreign field.

For a unified, Christian educational system.

For more hospitals, orphanages, homes, etc.

For a native ministry.

FOR THE HOME FIELD:

For work in the neglected centers of great cities and rural districts.

For statesmanship in giving freedom for unifying Christian work in community centers.

For courage to withdraw from a field that is overcrowded by other communions.

For work among foreigners, and prayer for all foreigners.

———

I delight to do thy will, O my God:
Yea, thy law is within my heart. Amen.
—*Psa. 40:8.*

———

O RIGHTEOUS FATHER, Creator and Redeemer of the world, but whom the world does not know, hear us as we come to thank Thee that Thou hast set before us the harvest field of the world. Be gracious to all missionaries in all nations, and clothe both them and those who send them with brotherly kindness, in order that alliances of friendship may be formed which shall lend new hope to the fulfilment of the commission for the evangelization of the world; through Jesus Christ our Lord. Amen.

[21]

Thursday

PRAYER FOR CHILD TRAINING AND EDUCATION

Train up a child in the way he should go: and when he is old, he will not depart from it.

—Prov. 22: 6.

———

Wisdom is the principal thing; therefore, get wisdom: and with all thy getting get understanding.

—Prov. 4: 7.

———

Ask, and it shall be given you; seek, and ye shall find; knock, and it shall be opened unto you: for every one that asketh receiveth; and he that seeketh findeth; and to him that knocketh it shall be opened.

—Matt. 7: 7, 8.

———

If ye abide in Me, and my words abide in you, ye shall ask what ye will, and it shall be done unto you. Herein is my Father glorified, that ye bear much fruit; so shall ye be my disciples.

—John 15: 7, 8.

———

When the fight begins within himself,
A man's worth something.
—ROBERT BROWNING. *Bishop Blougram's Apology.*

———

The act of praying is the very highest energy of which the human mind is capable; praying, that is, with the total concentration of the faculties. The great mass of worldly men and of learned men are absolutely incapable of prayer.

—COLERIDGE.

[22]

Thursday

PRAYER FOR CHILD TRAINING AND EDUCATION

FOR EDUCATIONAL WORK:

For children to get the right start in education.

For knowledge in spiritual and mental development.

For all educational instructors and authors of text-books.

For making the student to become something rather than to learn something.

FOR EDUCATIONAL OBLIGATION:

For the public to recognize the right of all children to be educated.

For proper financial appropriations and gifts to that end.

For persons of spiritual character to occupy the position of teachers.

For a large place in all education for the Great Teacher.

FOR EDUCATIONAL INSTITUTIONS:

For all schools—city, state, church, and private.

For healthful recreation in education.

For establishing unifying processes for all church schools and colleges.

For an education that will lead all into proper attitude toward classes, races, nations, and churches.

O send out thy light and thy truth; let them lead me:
Let them bring me unto thy holy hill,
And to thy tabernacles.
Then will I go unto the altar of God,
Unto God my exceeding joy;
Yea, upon the harp will I praise Thee, O God
my God. Amen.

—Psa. 43: 3, 4.

O LORD OUR GOD, bless the instructors in all educational institutions and that great multitude of students that are now passing through their most impressionable periods to maturity; through Jesus Christ our Lord. Amen,

[23]

Friday

PRAYER FOR ALL NATIONS

And hath made of one blood all nations of men for to dwell on all the face of the earth.

—Acts 17: 26.

———

I exhort, therefore, that, first of all, supplications, prayers, intercessions, and giving of thanks, be made for all men: For kings, and for all that are in authority; that we may lead a quiet and peaceable life in all godliness and honesty.

—I Tim. 2: 1, 2.

———

There is no principle of the heart that is more acceptable to God, than an universal fervent love to all mankind, wishing and praying for their happiness; because there is no principle of the heart that makes us more like God, who is love and goodness itself, and created all beings for their enjoyment of happiness.

—WILLIAM LAW. *A Serious Call.*

———

By words and works we can but teach or influence a few; by our prayers we may benefit the whole world, and every individual of it, high and low, friend, stranger, and enemy. Is it not fearful then to look back on our past lives even in this one respect?

How can we answer to ourselves for the souls who have, in our time, lived and died in sin . . . or those again who have died with but doubtful signs of faith, the death-bed penitent, the worldly, the double-minded, the ambitious, the unruly, the trifling, the self-willed, seeing that, for what we know, we were ordained to influence or reverse their present destiny, and have not done it?

—J. H. NEWMAN. *Parochial Sermons.*

Friday
PRAYER FOR ALL NATIONS

FOR THE NATIONS:

For the rulers of all nations,—especially for the President of the United States and the King of England and the rulers of the countries where we may be,—and all executives.

For the law-makers and legislatures.

For the judges and courts of justice.

For the people.

FOR INDUSTRIAL, CLASS, AND RACIAL AFFAIRS:

For persons engaged in agriculture, merchandising, commerce, manufactures, trades, professions, art, inventions, and discoveries.

For all brain and hand toilers.

For the adjustment of class and race problems.

For peace and prosperity by the way of Christ.

FOR INTERNATIONAL RELATIONS:

For all movements that help toward friendly attitudes among the nations.

For international conferences dealing with economic problems, etc.

For adjusting international disputes by reason rather than by physical force.

For the support of the international court by an international conscience.

———

Blessed is the nation whose God is the Lord,
And the people whom He hath chosen for his own inheritance.
Behold, the eye of the Lord is upon them that fear Him,
Upon them that hope in his mercy. Amen.
—Psa. 33: 12, 18.

———

O LORD, we beseech Thee for our nation and for all the nations of the world that they may grow toward Thee as the plants grow toward the sun. Give to all peoples minds schooled for fellowship with Thee, when the kingdoms of this world shall become the Kingdom of our Lord and his Christ. Amen.

[25]

𝕾𝖆𝖙𝖚𝖗𝖉𝖆𝖞

PRAYER FOR PERSONAL INTERESTS

For the eyes of the Lord are over the righteous, and his ears are open unto their prayers: but the face of the Lord is against them that do evil.

—I Pet. 3: 12.

Whatsoever ye shall ask in my name, that will I do, that the Father may be glorified in the Son. If ye shall ask anything in my name, I will do it. If ye love Me, keep my commandments.

—John 14: 13-15.

Against Thee, Thee only, have I sinned, and done this evil in thy sight.

—Psa. 51: 4.

There is nothing that makes us love a man so much as praying for him; and when you can once do this sincerely for any man, you have fitted your soul for the performance of everything that is kind and civil toward him.

—WILLIAM LAW. *A Serious Call.*

Pray for my soul. More things are wrought by
    prayer
Than this world dreams of. Wherefore, let thy
    voice
Rise like a fountain for me night and day.
For what are men better than sheep or goats
That nourish a blind life within the brain,
If, knowing God, they lift not hands of prayer
Both for themselves and those who call them friend?
For so the whole round earth is every way
Bound by gold chains about the feet of God.
—ALFRED TENNYSON. *The Passing of Arthur.*

Saturday

PRAYER FOR PERSONAL INTERESTS

FOR INDIVIDUALS:
  For friends and neighbours and benefactors.
  For enemies.
  For associates.
  For helpers in general and in special tasks.

FOR COÖPERATIVE MOVEMENTS:
  For those that are local—church, city, etc.
  For those that are wider—state, national, and international.
  For the leaders and workers in them.
  For their benefactors.

FOR SELF:
  For the things accomplished and the things in which we have failed.
  For the things that have hurt.
  For financial adjustments.
  For health of soul and body.

> Thou wilt show me the path of life:
> In thy presence is fulness of joy;
> At thy right hand there are pleasures for
>   evermore. Amen.
>
> —*Psa. 16: 11.*

OUR FATHER, we know not what to ask of Thee. Thou knowest what we need before we ask. Give us only that which Thou thinkest best. Cast us down or lift us up. We would have thy will done in us and in all those persons and movements that have our personal interests, and so we simply present ourselves before Thee and say, Thou art our Father, who art in heaven. Hallowed by thy name. Thy Kingdom come. Thy will be done in us; through Jesus Christ our Lord. Amen.

[27]

FAMILY WORSHIP [1]

Few things give more pleasure to our heavenly Father than for a family to pray to Him together. The best way, of course, is for every one to kneel down. But if that cannot be done, make the children stand, or sit, at the table with their eyes shut, before they begin breakfast, and after they have finished supper, while the father or mother conducts the brief service.

—A. H. McNEILE. *A Daily Offering.*

Where two or three are gathered together in my name, there am I in the midst of them.

—*Matt. 18: 20.*

He [Jesus] took Peter and John and James, and went up into a mountain to pray.

—*Luke 9: 28.*

Whosoever cometh to Me, and heareth my sayings, and doeth them, I will show you to whom he is like: He is like a man which built a house, and digged deep, and laid the foundation on a rock; and when the flood arose, the stream beat vehemently upon that house, and could not shake it; for it was founded upon a rock.

—*Luke 6: 47, 48.*

[1] If there is difficulty in getting the family together, that difficulty may be obviated by having a brief service at the breakfast table or at the evening meal. Only a few minutes need to be consumed by such a service, so that no one could object because of the lack of time. There are numerous manuals for this service, such as *Great Souls at Prayer,* by Mary W. Tileston, published by R. H. Allenson, Racquet Court, Fleet St., London, E. C., or Little, Brown & Co., Boston, $1.00; *The Daily Altar,* by H. L. Willett and C. C. Morrison, Christian Century, Chicago, $1.50; and *God's Minute,* by 365 Ministers and Laymen, Vir Publishing Co., Philadelphia, Pa., 50 cents.

FAMILY WORSHIP

A MORNING PRAYER:

ALMIGHTY GOD, who day by day renewest the face of nature, giving back again that which was lost; and who givest the bread of the body by which we are restored unto the vigour of life! Grant unto us, this day, such holy thoughts and pious meditations upon the words of the wise of olden times, and the words of thy Son our Lord, that they may be to us as food and water renewing our strength, deepening our hope, and fitting us for the struggle to make the spiritual life supreme. Hear us; through Jesus Christ our Lord. Amen.

—GEORGE DAWSON. *Prayers.*

———

AN EVENING PRAYER:

O God, whose blessed Son Jesus Christ came to give us the peace which the world cannot give, let thy peace rest upon our souls to-night, and the souls of those who love Thee in all the nations of the earth: through the same Jesus Christ our Lord. Amen.

—A. H. MCNEILE. *A Daily Offering.*

———

A PRAYER OF THANKSGIVING BEFORE MEALS:

O LORD, we pray for thy presence at this meal. If we have ever gained our bread by injustice, or eaten it in heartlessness, cleanse our life and give us a spirit of humility and love, that we may be worthy to sit at the common table of humanity in the great house of our Father. Amen.

—WALTER RAUSCHENBUSCH. *Prayers of the Social Awakening.*

———

A PRAYER OF THANKSGIVING AFTER MEALS:

BLESSED LORD, as we live continually upon thy bounty, so may we always live to thy glory: through Jesus Christ. Amen.

—*The Tent and the Altar.*

[29]

PRAYER PERIOD AT PENTECOST

The significance of Pentecost is emphasized by the outpouring of the Holy Spirit on that day (Acts 2). For ten days preceding that day, they "all continued with one accord in prayer and supplication" (Acts 1:14). It was a period of joyfulness. It may be made much more so in our present day experience. From Ascension to Pentecost many Christians in all parts of the world meet together for union in prayer.

———

And it shall come to pass in the last days, saith God, I will pour out of my Spirit upon all flesh: and your sons and your daughters shall prophesy, and your young men shall see visions, and your old men shall dream dreams: and on my servants and on my handmaidens I will pour out in those days of my Spirit; and they shall prophesy: and I will show wonders in heaven above, and signs in the earth beneath; blood, and fire, and vapour of smoke: The sun shall be turned into darkness, and the moon into blood, before that great and notable day of the Lord come: and it shall come to pass, that whosoever shall call on the name of the Lord shall be saved.
—Joel 2: 28-32; Acts 2: 17-21.

———

For the promise is unto you, and to your children, and to all that are afar off, even as many as the Lord our God shall call.
—Acts 2: 39.

PRAYER PERIOD AT PENTECOST

FIRST DAY:
  For an Understanding of God (Psa. 100:3).
SECOND DAY:
  For an Understanding of Jesus Christ (John 14:6).
THIRD DAY:
  For an Understanding of the Holy Spirit (Rom. 8:16).
FOURTH DAY:
  For an Understanding of the Kingdom of God
                                    (Matt. 6:33).
FIFTH DAY:
  For an Understanding of the Cross (Phil. 2:8).
SIXTH DAY:
  For an Understanding of Discipleship (John 13:35).
SEVENTH DAY:
  For an Understanding of Penitence (1 John 1:9).
EIGHTH DAY:
  For an Understanding of Thanksgiving
                                    (1 Thess. 5:18).
NINTH DAY:
  For an Understanding of Witnessing (Matt. 28:19, 20).
TENTH DAY:
  For an Understanding of Unity (John 17:21).

———

O LORD, by whose life we are made alive and by whose mercy we are blessed, live in us. Forgive our negligence. Blot out all our sins. Preserve in us a living faith. Shed abroad thy light in the hearts of all who pray. Make brotherhood among us a reality. Stir in our souls obedience to thy long ago given commission to make disciples of all the nations. So command us that we shall have the sense to know that the winning of the nations is dependent upon the unity of the Church. Comfort us with thy Spirit and so prepare our hearts that Thou mayest not be afraid to trust us with thy Spirit's power; through Jesus Christ our Lord. Amen.

"LIFT up your hearts "—" We lift them up "—
                    Ah me!
I cannot, Lord, lift up my heart to Thee:
Stoop, lift it up, that where Thou art I too may be.

"Give Me thy Heart "—I would not say Thee nay,
But have no power to keep or give away
My heart: stoop, Lord, and take it to thyself to-day.

Stoop, Lord, as once before, now once anew
Stoop, Lord, and hearken, hearken, Lord, and do,
And take my will, and take my heart, and take me
        too.

                    —CHRISTINA G. ROSSETTI (*Redeeming
                            the Time—S. P. C. K.*).

V

THE SCHOOL OF PRAYER

WHEN one of the disciples of Christ said to, Him, " Lord, teach us to pray, as John also taught his disciples " (Luke 11 : 1), it was the knock at the door for the opening of the school of prayer. Through the years, God had taken his children here and there and put them in the school of prayer, but now the time had come when the school was to be opened to all. Christ, at once, gave the first lesson and, after all these years, not many of us have learned it. That first lesson is that God is Father and we must, unconditionally, both reverence Him and put Him and his interests first, and ourselves and our interests second. It has always been difficult to establish in our attitudes that God is, really and eternally, Father, and it is still difficult; but our hearts must show this faith and our courtesy must manifest itself in making his interests first and in uniting our wills with his will. This is not only the politeness of prayer. It is the wisdom of prayer—(1) God is really Father; (2) we must reverence Him in his Living Presence; (3) we must recognize the Kingdom within us in the process of making; and (4) we must unify our wills with his will to complete

[33]

his work of creation. These principles are fundamental in spiritual experience.

What Christ gave us, in the opening of what is commonly called the Lord's Prayer, is an interpretation of the first of the ten commandments. Christ was constantly reiterating it. "Seek ye first the kingdom of God, and his righteousness" (Matt. 6:33). God is love; He is neither untrue nor unkind; therefore, He must be first. He knows our needs (Matt. 6:32). His interests include us, and He needs our heart and mind and will to bring to completion the unfinished creation. The things that He is doing and what He wants us to become are of more importance than our little plans and passing needs, be they ever so big in our own eyes.

He could not have left us a more satisfactory example of this idea than He did, when, in teaching us to pray, He said: " Our Father who art in heaven. Hallowed be thy name. Thy kingdom come. Thy will be done on earth as it is in heaven." Thus far, which includes nearly half of the prayer, it is concerned with God and his interests. Then, concerning ourselves—" Give us this day our daily bread, and forgive us our trespasses as we forgive those who trespass against us. Lead us not into temptation, but deliver us from evil." Then, back to God and his interests again—" For thine is the kingdom and the power and the glory for ever and ever. Amen." Although this last was an addition to the original text, and is, therefore, omitted in many translations; nevertheless, it is not inappropriate, inasmuch as it emphasizes the place of God.

The lesson is that of humility. It was among the first lessons that God taught the Hebrews (Deut. 8:2, 3). It was voiced by the prophets as one of the fundamental principles in proper living (Mic. 6:8). Both Old and New Testaments affirm God's reception of the humble (Prov. 3:34; Jas. 4:6). Christ repeatedly taught that exaltation comes by the way of humility (Luke 14:11), and Paul cites the case of Christ as fulfilling perfectly this sublime idea (Phil. 2:6–11) and exhorts Christians to its practice (Col. 3:12).

Only the humble soul can have communion with God. There is no other pathway of approach to the Living Presence. Out of humility the Psalmist says:

> Pour out your heart before Him:
> God is a refuge for us (62:8).

The one way to get rid of sin is to pour it out before God,—all sinful thoughts and actions,—making a complete confession of everything. We should prove to Him that we are committed to the cleansing of the heart, for God is a refuge for all.

The Psalmist again says:

> I have set the Lord always before me (16:8).

As wonderful as these words were in the experience of the Hebrews, how much more wonderful is it in the experience of Christians to find in Christ the

[35]

Living Way to the Father, having Him always before us.

And the Psalmist again says:

Unto Thee, O Lord, do I lift up my soul (25:1).

The lifting of the soul to God is an experience transcending in importance all other human activities. It is the touch of life upon life. It is the meeting place of Father and child, declaring an eternal kinship.

These three figures beautifully express the meaning of prayer—pouring out of the heart, setting the Lord before us, and the lifting up of our souls unto Him. No more picturesque and correct description of prayer can be found in any age, nor in any literature. They tell what prayer is without dropping to the level of a definition. They place it in those great spiritual realms of the poetic and picturesque. They bring into mutual association humility, resolution, and the consciousness of God. These are the essential elements of prayer. Combine these and prayer is, at once, simplified: but our difficulty lies in bringing these together. Pride halts humility, indecision halts resolution, and self-consciousness halts the consciousness of God. Nevertheless, we pray.

It is a natural and universal instinct. Prayers are among the earliest expression of language. Mothers in all ages have taught their children to pray as they have taught them to eat and to walk.

THE SCHOOL OF PRAYER

Although natural and simple, the experiences of prayer have been attended with many difficulties. To make prayer better—and the making of *better* prayers is more important than the making of many prayers—we meet the same difficulties that we find in attempting to attain to proficiency in music, or in languages, or in any of the trades or occupations of life. All these things are natural, but proficiency comes at the cost of labour—usually hard labour. " The call to prayer means a call to work, not a summons to set going a machine, which needs neither brains nor heart. It is a call to gather up all the forces of the soul, and to summon them to the intensest activity. It is, indeed, the highest exercise to which man can be called." [1]

The fact that prayer is natural and simple indicates that its development comes by skillful perseverance in its practice—not finding beautiful language, but practicing humility, resolution, and the consciousness of God. Multiplying times to pray, or resorting to devotional books, or searching out our personal needs, are superficial and secondary methods in removing difficulties in the way of prayer. We must learn the meekness and the lowliness of Christ. This is the method to which He invites us. " Come unto Me, all ye that labour and are heavy laden, and I will give you rest. Take my yoke upon you, and learn of Me; for I am meek

---

[1] James Hastings. *The Christian Doctrine of Prayer* (Clark).

and lowly in heart: and ye shall find rest unto your souls. For my yoke is easy, and my burden is light " (Matt. 11:28–30). The secret lies here. Consequently, another's knowledge of God is of the same kind of help to us as another's knowledge of music. Each must learn for himself.

The consciousness of God as the Living Father is the glory of prayer. It is this that quickens prayer and gives direction to it. The emphasis must be on Him—not on ourselves. It is our meeting ground with Him. There is a personal attitude on his part, or He could not hear and answer; there is a personal attitude on the part of ourselves, else there could be no sense of humility, no resolution, and no pouring out of the heart, no setting of the Lord always before us, and no lifting up of the soul to the Living Father. There is, then, a personal consciousness on the part both of God and of ourselves in our approach toward each other. But consciousness of God must not be associated with self-consciousness, which is destructive of truth and deadens our consciousness of God. The consciousness of our need may weaken prayer; our helplessness may drive us to pray; neither of these, however, is prayer. Prayer is the voice of reality within us, holding conversation with the Living Father, directing heart, mind, and will toward Him.

It is not the language of prayer that gives it force. It is the attitude of the soul toward God. The words of prayer may be very beautiful, but the

[38]

prayer itself may be very rude. The prayer may be read, or it may be an extemporaneous supplication; but, if there is no inner voice speaking to God, it is not prayer. The posture of the body is of secondary consequence. Belief is the level from which the soul comes naturally into the Living Presence. Then God and his interests are first, and the prayer conforms us truly to the Divine laws as the stars in their courses and the ocean in its tides.

In the school of prayer we must always keep near the great Teacher. It is profitable to go carefully through the four Gospels and classify all his statements and actions regarding prayer; then, test them, not once, but many times. Make our inner selves the laboratory. Perhaps it would be better to use the term temple, for we are the temple of the Living God, and God dwells in us and walks in us and calls us his own (II Cor. 6:16). Our problem is not without; it is within us. In spite of this fact God sometimes seems to be absent. Belief in an absentee God is the source of sin. But it is not true that He is absent, for He is always with us and within us. Nevertheless, in his seeming absence, we cry out with Job:

> Oh that I knew where I might find Him!
> That I might come even to his seat!
> I would set my cause in order before Him,
> And fill my mouth with arguments (23:3, 4, R. V.).

There are times when our prayers should be strong pleadings, sustained by Scripture, history, and experience. He pleads with us, saying: " Come now, and let us reason together " (Isa. 1 : 18) : we, in turn, plead with Him, saying in the language of the Jerusalem taxgatherer : " God be merciful to me a sinner " (Luke 18 : 13). We must know each other —God and ourselves.

Human friendship is based on knowledge and congeniality; it is likewise so in friendship between God and ourselves. God must be known as the Living Father by personal experience. James Hastings well says: " We get to know our friends better by conversation and familiar intercourse. And so shall we get to know God better by conversing with Him. But we are very apt to forget that, if the conversation is to do this work, it must not be one-sided; and our ordinary conversation with God is terribly one-sided. We insist on doing all the talking ourselves. We go straight through our prayer, without taking breath, and then get up and run away, without leaving a moment to God in which He may talk to us. It is no wonder that such prayers do not much advance our knowledge of Him, to whom we speak, and to whom we refuse to listen." [1]

A school means discipline. We should set ourselves to the practice of self-training in prayer as we practice in music, or in the apprenticeship of a

---

[1] James Hastings. *The Christian Doctrine of Prayer* (Clark).

trade. On the other hand, if we resort to the sloven method of going at it by snatches, we will never be proficient, whether it be prayer, or music, or a trade. There must be deliberate, painstaking care. We will frequently be discouraged in our practicing of humility, resolution, and the consciousness of God, as we are in the practice of other things that have to do with proficiency. But they who care will continue to pursue their tasks. These are the world builders, whether they be working in the field of physical or spiritual values. " To him that overcometh will I give to eat of the tree of life, which is in the midst of the paradise of God " (Rev. 2:7).

In the study of prayer we are for ever face to face with the two great spiritual facts — Incarnation and Redemption. In one Jesus made the complete identification of God with us and, in the other, He released God's free gift of eternal life. The many theories about these facts may differ, and necessarily do differ, but their difference need not confuse us, for the facts are as sure as the sun. Both our experience and hope are grounded in them. No theories can take them away from us. They are as much a part of us as memory, reason, and expectation. In the contemplation of them the consciousness of God is deepened in us and prayer becomes the first of faith's activities, whence we venture in new discoveries from which come spiritual refreshment in a stronger faith and a more compre-

hensive love. The one thing which distinguishes
Christianity from other religions is the kind of redemption it offers to mankind, which is a redemption based on reconciliation. In other religions renunciation is first and reconciliation follows:
whereas, in Christianity, reconciliation is first and
renunciation gets its power and direction from
reconciliation, which Christianity offers. Prayer is
the channel of its accomplishment.

Prayer is the source of all godliness. Out of its
school we are graduated for waiting service in the
Kingdom of God. We have not been left to
stumble in the dark. The Light of the world is
here. Christ says: " He that hath seen Me hath
seen the Father " (John 14:9). He has simplified
three great experiences—(1) Repentance, teaching
us to be unashamed of it; (2) Confession, teaching
us the faithfulness and justice of God in forgiving
all sin; and (3) Perseverance, teaching us of the
possibilities of growth into the likeness of Himself.
Undergirding these is belief, growing with each
adventure. These experiences give reality to the
pouring out of the heart, to the setting of the Lord
always before us, and to the lifting up of the soul
to the Living Father, who loves us and is ever calling us into the school of prayer.

O Thou Teacher of Mankind, grant us an entrance into the school of prayer that we may learn the wondrous art of tarrying behind the closed door with thyself and us alone. Teach us humility, resolution, and the consciousness of thyself that we may always make Thee first in our thoughts. Thou didst press upon us the atmosphere of thy heart to make us want what Thou wantest us to have. Neither the consciousness of our needs nor the helplessness of our condition is presented to Thee for our prayer, but out of humility of heart and mind and will, we lift up our souls to Thee, and call Thee Father, confessing our penitence, rejoicing in our fellowship, and believing that Thou wilt supply our needs and sustain us in our helplessness; through Jesus Christ our Lord. Amen.

O GOD, help me to believe in Thee. I need Thee to keep me loyal to the great realities of truth and goodness, of love and righteousness, to strengthen my will for the fulfilment of every duty, and to enable me to disbelieve my fears and to trust my hopes. Reveal thyself to me as my soul's Companion and Friend. Only let me know that Thou art with me, and I will face the worst that may befall, knowing that all things—suffering and adversity as well as joy and well-being—work together for good to them that love Thee. Set me free from every restraining care and anxiety, that I may give myself without reserve to the doing of thy will, and so come to know thy peace. Amen.

—SAMUEL MCCOMB (*A Book of Prayers—Dodd, Mead & Co.*).

VI

THE REALITY OF PRAYER

GOD is real. Man is real. It would be unthinkable to suppose that the Creator had provided no method of communication between these two great realities, but instead both were forever to remain in isolated splendour. Consequently, the reality of prayer is a natural conclusion. From the earliest times men have prayed. In these times the greatest interpreters of life are those who pray.

We cannot use prayer like we use the telephone and the telegraph, by pushing a button or ringing a bell. The machinery may be perfectly constructed, yet if there is some broken connection,—although it may be only the width of a hair,—neither the telephone nor the telegraph will be able to command the service of electricity. Science has found the physical law in one instance; faith must find the spiritual law in the other instance. These laws are similar—so similar that we are being constantly reminded of a close analogy between them. Both are Divine. The face of the earth has been changed by Christianity, the power of advance of which has depended upon prayer. This has been done, too, with a mild and defective form of Christianity. If faith had been as venturesome in the field of spiritual experience as the scientific working has been in the physical field, our material civilization would not only rest upon a more permanent spiritual basis, but the ideals of the Kingdom would be nearer their fulfilment. The spiritual, however, has been difficult and costly. But, even as it is, the desire for prayer is foremost in the reality of human experience.

It was certainly a great force in the life of Christ and in the lives of the saints of the Scriptures and of history. Miss Maude Royden says: " Prayer is, at least, as real and living a force in the world as any of the great forces revealed to us by Natural Science. It seems to most of us capricious and unreliable for the same reason that, for example, electricity seemed so to a world which knew it only as flashes of lightning or sparks from a black cat: namely, that we do not understand its nature or its laws. When we do so, we shall be able to pray with power, as Christ did and all the saints in their degree. We shall share his perfect confidence and we shall understand that we ' have not because we ask not.' " [1] It is to-day the most urgent field of exploration and adventure. Both in science and commerce faith is making such wonderful ventures as to place its results almost in the realm of the miraculous, while in religion faith is less free. It shies at ventures, leaving spiritual ex-

[1] A. Maude Royden. *Prayer as a Force* (Putnam).

THE REALITY OF PRAYER

perience without those results that should exceed
the results in either science or commerce.

The reality does not rest upon our needs nor our
desires, but upon God. Prayer is God's breathing
in the soul of man, sometimes expressed in petition,
or in penitence, or in thanksgiving, or in meditation,
or in intercession, or in adoration. None of these
are in themselves prayer. They are the channels
through which prayer finds its outlets to God.
Prayer uses these as we use the multiplication table,
or grammar. Back of these are the sources of
prayer and those sources are in God. It is inter-
estingly true that as these spiritual impressions come
from God, there is, likewise, a spiritual power that
takes our ignorant prayers and unspoken longings
and translates them into Divine idealism in the heart
of God. " Thus also the Spirit helps us in our
weakness. For we do not know what to pray for as
we ought, but the Spirit itself intercedes for us with
sighs beyond words " (Rom. 8 : 26).[1]

Prayer puts us in fellowship with all the saints—
that vast multitude that has finished the battle—
who, by the Spirit of God, have overcome every
foe, and are now in unobstructed fellowship with
Christ. Paul was able to say: " Having a desire
to depart, and to be with Christ; which is
far better " (Phil. 1 : 23). And, then, that
other multitude in all communions, in all parts

----

[1] Riverside Translation.

of the world, to whom angels minister in order that all may overcome by the power of Christ as Christ Himself was ministered to by angels (Mark 1 : 13; Luke 22 : 43). "Are they [angels] not all ministering spirits, sent forth to minister for them who shall be heirs of salvation?" (Heb. 1 : 14). Prayer brings all ages into fellowship, more influential in permanent results than the telegraph or telephone, which has transformed the present age into a whispering gallery and which is a parable of the wide function of prayer. We pray to God. We are mysteriously influenced by the prayers of all the past and all the present. The communion of saints is real.

Nevertheless, multitudes of Christians are haunted by the unreal in prayer. They go through the form and, perhaps, never miss a day in saying their prayers, but saying prayers and praying are two different things. Prayer is friendship between two personalities, and the law of friendship binds to each the consciousness of the other, the knowledge of the other, and personal transactions between each other.

The reality of prayer is dependent upon the degree of our coöperation with God. We can block every approach by refusing or neglecting to cultivate faith. "Without faith it is impossible to please Him; for he that cometh to God must believe that He is, and that He is a rewarder of them that diligently seek Him" (Heb. 11 : 6). Likewise, refusing to break away our attachment for some one sin. "If I regard iniquity in my heart, the Lord will not hear me" (Psa. 66: 18). Unfaith or one sin knowingly unrepented of is sufficient to prevent our experiencing the reality of prayer. Faith must be cultivated and sins must be abandoned.

Words are useful to us, but in prayer words are not the primary things. Back of all words, and that which speaks louder than words, is the attitude of the soul toward God. Sometimes it is difficult for us to know our own attitude. Sometimes the words we use in prayer are far beyond what we are really willing to pay the price for. Sometimes our minds are so divided or confused that we are not sure of what we want. All these things are human conditions, common the world over and through all ages, but that does not justify our indefiniteness, thoughtlessness, or indecision. But back of all words is the real person—frequently so far back that the person does not comprehend himself. Nevertheless, it is the voice of reality that God hears above the voice of audibility. The transaction is in that realm rather than any other. There the prayer is answered. Perhaps, we do not recognize the answer. But it remains true now as of old: "According to your faith be it unto you" (Matt. 9: 29).

One of the greatest hindrances against experiencing the reality of prayer is our self-will in trying to get God to do what we want Him to do,—purely a pagan idea,—instead of surrendering in absolute obedience to Him, thereby having Him to do what He wants to do with us. A friendship in which we are ever trying to get something and never giving anything is artificial. It is not a question, How many prayers has God answered for us? But rather in our friendship with God, How much have we grown like Him? We may lose property, social position, health, and loved ones, during which time we prayed earnestly for God's help; but, if in all this defeat and sorrow, we have grown toward God, our growth is the evidence of the reality of prayer, for the building of souls on the foundations of God is the greatest thing in human experience.

We think of mankind as one, however varied and separated by great barriers; and, at the same time, we think of mankind as the instrument of God's expression, a kind of medium through which God speaks and reveals Himself. A. H. McNeile says: " Personality has been defined as 'the capacity for fellowship,' that is the capacity for self-communication to persons, communion, mutual response, mutual indwelling, real union, with persons. So that I am able to say—God is in me; God is in you. But remember, all idea of locality must be avoided. It is not a little bit of God inside me, and a little bit of God inside you, any more than we can say that there is a little bit of music inside one violin and a little bit of music inside another violin. It is God, the one infinite reality, who reveals Him-

THE REALITY OF PRAYER

self as physical life in all nature, and as personal character in man. The twofold truth is stated in the Prologue of the Fourth Gospel: 'All things were made by Him, and without Him was not anything made that was made; in Him was Life.' Thus far the evangelist describes reality in Nature. But then comes the leap to the higher plane: 'The Life was the Light of men.' That is what makes all mankind one. As individuals, men are only instruments, symbols, 'parables,' to use Goethe's word, of the Infinite and the Eternal. But as personal, mankind is one communion and fellowship. And the more we can annul our individual Self, the more free we are to realize our oneness with the whole. He that loseth his Self shall find it." [1]

Only in the reality of prayer is self lost. But prayer is not merely conforming to an established custom, be it public or private. It is not a ritual; it is an experience. In its practice we become a part of the great circle of God and human souls, both in the past and in the present. Prayer is to us either a matter of little consequence or of great value, depending entirely upon the degree of our experimentation in it. The bigness of prayer dawns upon us only when we have had a great experience in its practice.

Take a simple illustration like the hyacinth. Neither a botanist nor a biologist could tell us what

---

[1] A. H. McNeile. *Self-Training in Prayer* (Longmans).

a hyacinth really is. Not until we have seen it for ourselves do we really know. Books and sermons are to prayer what the botanist and biologist are to the hyacinth. The reality of prayer must come out of experience. In the fellowship of the personal soul with the personal God prayer flows out of petition and thanksgiving and such like channels into the expanding of the human life through the processes of the Divine fellowship.

In our thought of God as personal and ourselves as persons, we are brought to the reality of communion and fellowship between Him and us. Our approaches may be defective, due to our ignorance and self-will, but the approaches have gone on through the centuries as positively as the rising and the setting of the sun, so that the history of prayer is as old as mankind, and the benefits of prayer have been the oldest heritage of the race.

O LORD OF LOVE, Thou art real. Deepen our experiences in the reality of our communion with Thee, lest we disappoint both ourselves and Thee, and lose the aliveness of prayer. Touch the artificial and unreal in us that all barrenness may be supplanted by things that bloom. Thou preparest the heart; then prepare our hearts by such sincerity and humility of approaches that all vain phrases and artificial attitudes may give way to vividity and reality. We need Thee. Breathe into us heavenly desires and may no resistance of ours hinder the work of thy free Spirit within us, for the sake of Him, who is the Lord of Life. Amen.

Thou who wouldest have every man provide for his own
house, and who hatest the unnatural,
Remember, Lord, my kinsmen according to the flesh;
grant me to speak peace concerning them, and to seek
their good.

Thou who wouldest that our righteousness should exceed
the righteousness of sinners,
Grant me, Lord, to love those who love me, my own
friends, and my father's friends, and never to forsake
my friends' children.

Thou who wouldest that we should overcome evil with
good, and pray for those who persecute us,
Have pity on mine enemies, Lord, as on myself; and bring
them together with me to thy heavenly Kingdom.

Thou who grantest the prayers of thy servants one for
another,
Remember, Lord, for good, and pity all those who remember me in their prayers, all those whom I have
promised to remember in mine.

—W. H. Frere and A. L. Illingworth (*Sursum
Corda—Mowbray*).

VII

THE PROFESSION OF PRAYER

THERE are instances of individuals giving themselves to prayer, as of the Psalmist, who said: "I give myself unto prayer" (Psa. 109:4); but not until the Apostles of Christ gave themselves continually to prayer do we find prayer passing into a profession. "It is not reason that we should leave the word of God, and serve tables (meals),"[1] said the Apostles; "but we will give ourselves continually to prayer, and to the ministry of the word" (Acts 6:2, 4).

Every theological institution should have a chair in the study of and training in prayer, including spiritual discipline and "the exploration of the interior life of prayer and union with God in all its wondrous heights and depths." It is as important to have such a chair as it is to have a chair in New Testament exegesis or homiletics. If it were a matter of rating, it would not be out of place to say that such a chair should have equal consideration with the chair of New Testament exegesis and homiletics. But we have treated prayer about as we have treated the sex problem; that is, it is a

---

[1] Moffatt's Translation.

delicate matter, not to be discussed too intimately, but each must stumble ahead and find out for himself. This policy in prayer has made both the pulpit and the pew weak in prayer, and frequently has given to our ministry a leanness and superficiality, irrespective of its theological training; and, in the sex problem, it has given us an inexcusable social scourge. One has to contend as severely for the place of prayer in his life as a sensual nature has to contend for purity in his thought and conduct.

Prayer must be taken out of its formal setting—however elegant our prayers may be—and be made a living experience, before we can be brought to command our wills to give ourselves to prayer. Having done this, we might write on the fly-leaf of our Bible, as John Wesley did on his: " Live To-day." Christ teaches us to live day by day. The past is gone. To-day is God's gift to us, whether it be a day of storm or sunshine. To-morrow may never come, and that is immaterial. In the event, however, that it does come, having lived right to-day, we are better prepared to live properly to-morrow.

The day may begin with the morning sacrifice. In his exhortation, Paul says: " I beseech you, brethren, by the mercies of God, that ye present your bodies a living sacrifice, holy, acceptable unto God, which is your reasonable service " (Rom. 12:1). It is beautifully appropriate to rise from our beds with the thought of God and with the presentation to the Lord of our bodies as "a living sacrifice," saying as we do so: "I laid me down and slept; I awaked; for the Lord sustained me" (Psa. 3:5); and, in the evening when we retire, to say some such passage as, "I will both lay me down in peace, and sleep: for Thou, Lord, only makest me dwell in safety" (Psa. 4:8).

A world-wide practice among many is to keep the Morning Watch. It may be very early. Of Christ it was said: "In the morning, rising up a great while before day, He went out, and departed into a solitary place, and there prayed" (Mark 1:35). It may be later in the day, only it should be before breakfast, and especially before reading the morning paper. Having spent that time in waiting before God, by Bible reading, meditation, and prayer, we are better prepared to adjust ourselves through the day to God's children, whom we meet in business and social circles. John R. Mott says: "In the light of experience and observation one may say with conviction that there is no habit more calculated to preserve the sense of reality in faith, to maintain and augment spiritual energy, and to prepare one for recognizing and heeding dangers and opportunities than that of beginning each day in this way." [1]

There will be times when we are hurried; but, if

---

[1] John R. Mott. *Confronting Young Men With the Living Christ* (Association).

we rise earlier in order to give sufficient time to our Morning Watch, we will discover in ourselves an assurance that we could hardly have possessed without such a practice.

The principles of discipline must control us in secret prayer as in other things. Difficulties can only be overcome when we will to conform to the mind of Christ. H. C. G. Moule says: " I would say, first, that the special difficulty of secret prayer is in the peculiar temptation to laxity and indolence in the practice, just because it is secret. In the case of public prayer, and social prayer, the fact of association brings of course a certain aid in this direction. We are constrained by it to keep time with others, at least to some degree, and to behave ourselves as men under the eyes of others. But we may shorten our time of secret prayer, we may thrust it into a corner, we may lie late in the morning, or sit up comfortably late at night, and we are seen by no eye that we can see, and we have no one to be offended by our absence, lateness, or carelessness. I am sure my reader knows, or has known, the reality of at least some such temptations. The warm bed when we wake,· the bright fire in the late evening, the allurements of book, or conversation, or whatever it is that *must give way* if we are to set ourselves to seek the King's face before we sleep, the specious excuses and palliations of the heart—these things are real, and they are peculiar hindrances to the full exercise of regular secret prayer. We intend to be up betimes, to meet God before we meet man. But, perhaps, our first meeting with God will be at family worship in the home, or at the chapel service in the college; and something whispers that this will do duty instead of the Morning Watch alone. *It will not do so.*[1]

Devotional books are helpful toward self-training in the profession of prayer. Many of these, from which quotations are made in this book, are purposely mentioned, giving the author, the title, and the publisher. But for this training there is but one book, and that is the Bible. A day is lost in which our hearts are not opened to the word of God. The Psalms, some of the great statements from the prophets, the words of Christ and Paul, in fact, all of the New Testament, ought to be read and reread, meditated on, thought over and over, until their living truths have penetrated into the heights and depths of our being. If we would understand the truth we must live the truth. Our lives must be saturated with it. It is said in *Theologia Germanica:* " No one can be made perfect in a day. A man must begin by denying himself, and willingly forsaking all things for God's sake, and must give up his own will, and all his natural inclinations, and separate and cleanse himself thoroughly from all sins and evil ways. After this, let him humbly take up the cross and follow Christ.

---

[1] H. C. G. Moule. *Secret Prayer* (Seely, London).

Also let him take and receive example and instruction, reproof, counsel, and teaching from devout and perfect servants of God, and not follow his own guidance. Thus the work shall be established and come to a good end. And when a man hath thus broken loose from and outleaped all temporal things and creatures, he may afterward become perfect in a life of contemplation. For he who will have the one must let the other go. There is no other way." [1]

He who makes prayer a profession will not talk about it. True humility will lead him to close his " inner chamber " to all except God and himself. As to what degree one has given himself to the profession of prayer, that must be discovered, in his conduct, by others. Two things remain to be mentioned in the self-training. These are (1) Finding refreshment in retreats, such as discussed in another chapter in this book, and (2) seeking to win others to Christ. There is no value in making prayer a profession if it does not include making " disciples of all the nations."

---

[1] G. W. McCalla, Philadelphia.

GRACIOUS GOD, we entreat thy mercy that Thou wilt set us free from all sins that doth so easily beset us. Let us look into the face of no man nor woman, nor child, be they rich or poor, acquaintance or stranger, friend or foe, white or coloured, but that we shall be able to wish them, from the depths of our hearts, the mercy of our God, who is the Father of all. Grant that we may so comprehend prayer as to give ourselves faithfully to its practice. Guide our vision in order that we may not only see in all the evidence of God's children, but may we have the grace to call forth that evidence until it be seen by all. Make all our faculties servants to thy will, until we shall have the consciousness that we are the trustees of thy goodness. Give us humility, diligence, and courage in dealing with ourselves, as well as in dealing with others, and receive the lifting up of our souls unto Thee, in the name of Him who loved us and gave Himself for us, even Jesus Christ, our Lord. Amen.

O GOD, who dost govern the thoughts of men; bring to
my mind the Upper Room where the Lord Jesus broke the
bread with his disciples in the night before He was crucified; grant to me that, being of that company, I may look
into the face of Him who gave Himself for the world.
While I eat of his bread and drink of his cup, fill my life
with his life, and send me forth to think his thoughts, to
say his words, to do his deeds; and so, O blessed Father,
grant that, though I know it not, the light of his face may
shine in my face, and all men may take note that I have
been with Jesus; who liveth and reigneth with Thee and
the Holy Spirit, the God of everlasting love, world without
end. Amen.

    —CHARLES LEWIS SLATTERY (*Prayers for Private and
       Family Use—Macmillan*).

VIII

FELLOWSHIP IN PRAYER

THERE is no field so abounding in romance as prayer. In dealing with some of its aspects, the author of *The Riches of Prayer*[1] intimates that he might appropriately call one of the chapters "The Romance of Prayer." What vast fields of exploration in prayer! What infinite variety of experiences! What great distances fill the vision of the soul! What new discoveries of God and self! There is no field in human experience just like it. World travel grows monotonous, but no one can explore continually into the field of prayer without experiencing perpetual joy. This is enhanced by fellowship in prayer.

Christ taught his disciples to pray in their inner chamber—this is individual prayer—and, likewise, He taught them to pray together—this is corporate prayer, which became the common practice of the early Church. "If two of you shall agree on earth as touching any thing that they shall ask, it shall be done for them of my Father who is in heaven. For where two or three are gathered together in my name, there am I in the midst of them" (Matt. 18: 19, 20). Corporate prayer must have deeply impressed the early disciples, for, at

---

[1] Longmans.

FELLOWSHIP IN PRAYER

Pentecost, it is said: " They were all with one accord in one place " (Acts 2:1). " These all continued with one accord in prayer and supplication " (Acts 1:14). And, later, those "that believed were of one heart and of one soul" (Acts 4:32). This is the very essence of corporate prayer. Whatever may have been their differences in background, environment, and temperament, their thoughts were centered on the purposes of God.

The path of fellowship is through prayer. It has in it the permanent spiritual basis. Christ said more in prayer about the unity of his followers than He ever said in public discourse (John 17). So long as we keep the order reversed there will be uncertain progress in the unity of Christendom. Corporate prayer is the method of understanding and friendship. When four or five persons, each representing a different communion, have got together in prayer, taking with them in their prayer the fact that Christ is in their midst, as He said He would be, it is likely that they will go away much closer together than if they had spent the time discussing their differences or their agreements. Corporate prayer is the path to permanent fellowship —not necessarily the only path, but the path of abundant hope. It establishes comradeship between personalities, making for oneness in will, faith, and purpose. If, however, one discovers aversion toward, or feels unfree in, praying with Christians of other Scriptural interpretation than his own, he is, to say the least, self-condemned, if not involved in moral insincerity, which Jesus frequently and severely condemned in the ecclesiastics of his time.

In corporate prayer there should be variety of temperaments and opinions, rather than uniformity. The world is crowded with variety and is upheld by the unity in God. It should be so with us in our fellowship one with another. Our differences should be no more disturbing than are oaks and elms in the forest, or tulips and carnations in the garden. We must learn that the beauty and strength of fellowship is in the combining of variety. The method for this is through corporate prayer. Uniformity and isolation are deadening attitudes, which are artificial and unspiritual; whereas, fellowship in prayer gives vitality and power to the fulfilment of the Divine purposes. It touches every discord, irregularity, and chasm in human life with the hope of peace, understanding, and good-will.

There must be the lifting up of the soul with willingness both to be untaught and taught, and with patience both to wait for instruction and to do as instructed, however difficult it may be. The whole process demands determination, humility, and patience. It may be a humiliating path we are to walk, or a heavy cross we are to carry, but these are the prices we pay for fellowship in prayer. The one purpose is to find the will of God by a united judgment. As far back as 1914 I came in touch with the Free Church Fellowship in England and the Anglican Fellowship. This kind of fellowship has in it wisdom and power, and means the re-vivifying of the spiritual life. In *Christian Fellow-ship in Thought and Prayer* it is said: " A company of men and women meet together that they may seek that richer consciousness of God, and, with it, that clearer light upon truth or conduct, their need of which has been impressed upon them. The first requirement is that their power of receptivity shall be intensified. Of God's willingness to lead them there is no question. The only point of uncertainty is in their ability to discern and to respond to his direction. Therefore, they will begin with earnest and united prayer. This prayer will not be hur-ried; it will be a sustained act of communion. And, therein, they will desire four things. First, they will together wait in silence for a more vivid sense of God's Presence and Reality. In the strain and bustle of ordinary life the vision of the Unseen may easily grow dim; they will tarry in stillness before God, craving the penitence and cleansing through which it may once more be made clear to them. Next, they will together pray for the coming of the Kingdom. This will be no light and easy intercession; they will reverently strive to view men from God's own standpoint, and, so far as may be, to enter into his sorrow for the world's sin and his sympathy with the world's need. And, when they have thus learnt a little less imperfectly to see mankind as God sees it, alike in its transgressions and in its ultimate possibilities, they will at last be ready, in the third place, to ask for light on the particular matter in which they need the Divine illumination. They will, therefore, pray together that in this special situation God's own design may be made plain to them. Lastly, that all hindrance in themselves may be removed, they will seek, before they turn to examine the problem, to be freed from every form of self-assertion. In the consciously-realized Presence of God, and relying on his aid, they will try to expel from their minds all previous bias, all personal preferences, and all self-seeking motives, and, at whatever cost, to will God's will both for themselves and for the world.

" This prayer, it is important to observe, is offered in an atmosphere of fellowship. The group of men engaged is more than a mere collection of individuals; it is a body of believers—a small but essential section of that living organism which is the Church of Christ, Himself its living Head. On this account the entire spiritual 'efficiency alike of every part and of the whole is immeasurably increased. Because of its mystical union with its fellows and with the Head, each separate member acquires a power never possessed and never attainable in isolation. The prayer of each, his penitence, his consecration, his very experience of God's Presence, is deepened and enriched by those of all; and, in its turn, ' through that which every joint

supplieth ' the entire body is itself built up in love.
This is no idle dream of what might be; it is a
statement of what actually takes place. And it is
in this atmosphere of a fellowship, both real and
realized, that those who employ the method we interpret are first made ready for the revelation of
God's will." [1]

In corporate prayer Christ is particularly clear
relative both to the Divine response and to identi-
fying Himself with the group (Matt. 18: 19, 20).
The experiences of the early disciples confirm this.
Consequently, it is not a venture into the field of
uncertainty. "Therefore, I say unto you, What
things soever ye desire, when ye pray, believe that
ye receive them, and ye shall have them" (Mark
11: 24). But this must be real prayer—not a self-
willed supplication; but, instead, such sense of reality as to involve labour, penitence, humility, and
obedience. It is not a process of ten or fifteen
minutes. Corporate prayer requires both work and
time. The answer may be "Yes" or "No," or
"Wait," or, more likely, it is altogether possible
that it will be the opposite of what we at first desired, for, in our fellowship with God, our desires
are modified or absolutely changed. The chief purpose of fellowship in prayer is to establish a highway for the will of God to be done on earth as it is
in heaven. This mutual fellowship is based on the

---

[1] Basil Mathews and Harry Bisseker. *Christian Fellowship in Thought and Prayer* (Gorham).

FELLOWSHIP IN PRAYER

common relationship to God, which is a relationship realized in a common fellowship among God's children. Hence, prayer becomes the intercourse of God's family, wherein all are brethren and God is Father.

———

O THOU LOVER OF FELLOWSHIP, grant us wisdom, we pray Thee, to find the fellowship of souls in prayer and to maintain this fellowship, knowing that, if it be but two or three, Thou art with us. Sanctify our powers of body and mind to the task of fellowship. Let us grow in faith and hope and love. Our hearts are open toward Thee; therefore, abide freely within us and make us thy temple wherein thy voice shall be heard perpetually as we seek to find the way toward each other. Give us a passion for corporate prayer and deny us not a united judgment under thy guidance; through Jesus Christ our Lord. Amen.

O Thou Eternal Love, whom Jesus has taught us to call our Father, and in whom we are learning to trust as our Brother, our Comrade, our Closest Friend, we are not seeking Thee. for we know that Thou art nearer to us every moment than we are to ourselves; we are only wishing and hoping that often, through this day, the thought of thy nearness to us, of thy presence with us, may spring into our consciousness, that we may see what Thou art showing us, and know what Thou art telling us, and be ready to take what Thou art giving us, and to do what Thou art bidding us.

Help us to feel more than once to-day that the good thoughts and the good wishes which we find in our hearts are signs of thy presence there; and may we learn to look for Thee thus, within our own lives, and to rejoice when we find Thee there, and so to become aware, more and more, of what we mean when we speak of the. fellowship and communion of the Holy Spirit! We know that Thou art working in us to will and to do thy good pleasure; and we know that Thou findest thy good pleasure in lives made fruitful and beautiful in thy service. So help us to work with Thee, this day and every day; through Jesus Christ, our Lord. Amen.

—Washington Gladden (*God's Minute—Vir Co.*).

IX

HINDRANCES IN PRAYER

PRAYER is difficult—to most of us very difficult. It is not difficult to say a prayer, whether it be read or extemporaneous; but it is difficult to experience the reality of the soul's communion with God, and, in the consciousness of his Presence, to direct our prayer toward Him.

The greatest hindrance, which we meet at the very outset, is that not many of us have much faith in prayer. We go through the form and are haunted by its unreality. In many instances we have not as much faith in our God as the pagan has in his god. Christian unfaith has made uncertain the road over which prayer travels to God. There is no conditon so serious in the Christian world to-day as the real value we put upon prayer. The whole Church is at a discount in this matter. Our unuse of Divine power, which we sorely need, cannot be corrected except by penitence and humility, for God has decreed that prayer should be, " a *power* in the universe, as distinct, as real, as natural, and as uniform, as the power of gravitation, or of light, or of electricity," says Austin Phelps. " A man may *use* it, as trustingly and as soberly as he would use either of these. It is as truly the dictate

of good sense, that a man should expect to achieve
something by praying, as it is that he should expect
to achieve something by a telescope, or the mariner's
compass, or the electric telegraph." [1] But before
one can use the telescope, or the compass, or the
telegraph, he must be trained in their use.

Underlying all hindrances of approach to God is
sin, which extends over a wide field. It may be
that of the tongue with its deceit, flattery, exaggera-
tion, slander, half-truths, and scurrilous talk. It
may be that of temper, uncharitable judgments, un-
fair criticisms, sensual thoughts, and harbouring of
a grudge. It may be in the conduct as to attitude,
finances, pride, secret sins, and superficiality. It
all may be summed up in the words of the Apostle:
" Now you know full well the doings of our lower
natures. Fornication, impurity, indecency, idol-
worship, sorcery; enmity, strife, jealousy, outbursts
of passion, intrigues, dissensions, factions, envying,
hard drinking, riotous feasting, and the like. And
as to these I forewarn you, as I have already fore-
warned you, that those who are guilty of such things
will have no share in the Kingdom of God " (Gal.
5 : 19–21). [2]

We cannot saunter into the Living Presence without preparation, which includes self-examination,
penitence, humility, decision, and obedience. Harry

[1] Austin Phelps. *The Still Hour* (Lothrop, Lee &
Shepard Co.).
[2] Weymouth's Translation.

HINDRANCES IN PRAYER

Emerson Fosdick says: " Let some debauché from
the dens of a city walk into a company where men
are chivalrous and women pure, and how much will
the debauché understand of his new environment?
Stone walls are not so impenetrable as the veil of
moral difference between the clean and the unclean.
So spiritual alienation between God and man makes
fellowship impossible. Of all the evils that most
surely work this malign result in man's communion
with the Father, the Master specially noted two:
impurity—' Blessed are the pure in heart, for *they*
shall see God ' (Matt. 5:8); and *vindictiveness,*
the unbrotherly spirit that will not forgive nor seek
to be forgiven—' If, therefore, thou art offering thy
gift before the altar, and there rememberest that
thy brother hath ought against thee, leave there thy
gift before the altar, and go thy way, first be recon-
ciled to thy brother, and then come and offer thy
gift ' (Matt. 5: 23, 24). *No one can be wrong with
man and right with God.* In Coleridge's *Ancient
Mariner,* one of the most vivid pictures of sin's
consequences evei drawn, the effect of lovelessness
on prayer, is put into a rememberable verse:

> " ' I looked to heaven and tried to pray,
>   But or ever a prayer had gush't,
> A wicked whisper came and made
>   My heart as dry as dust.' " [1]

Formality is a serious hindrance to real prayer.

[1] Harry Emerson Fosdick. *The Meaning of Prayer*
(Association).

HINDRANCES IN PRAYER

With it goes aimlessness, intellectual indolence, and unexamined lives. Instead of leading to humility and sincerity, which is one of the purposes of prayer, these lead to spiritual pride and hypocrisy. In the brief words of Christ we find nothing so severely condemned as this. It gives to the soul an unnatural attitude and deadens its functioning privileges with God. As a correction to wandering thoughts and tediousness in prayer, Jeremy Taylor says: " Pray often, and you will pray oftener; and when you are accustomed to a frequent devotion, it will so insensibly unite to your nature and affections, that it will become trouble to omit your usual or appointed prayers; and what you obtain at first by doing violence to your inclinations, at last will not be left without as great unwillingness as that by which at first it entered. This rule relies not only upon reason derived from the nature of habits, which turn into a second nature, and make their actions easy, frequent, and delightful; but it relies upon a reason depending upon the nature and constitution of grace, whose productions are of the same nature with the parent, and increases itself, naturally growing from grains to huge trees, from minutes to vast proportions, and from moments to eternity." [1]

Fear is the nightmare in experience. It is the lifetime bondage of many souls (Heb. 2: 15). In

---

[1] Jeremy Taylor. *Holy Living* (Longmans).

the bondage of this fear, we hesitate to venture out on the promises of God, testing their reality and satisfying the hope within us. We frequently start out all right, but, like Simon Peter, we begin to sink in the waters of our self-consciousness. Nevertheless, the Christ, whose outstretched arm saved the Apostle, saves us when, by faith, we behold his Living Presence, and call upon Him to set us free from our lifetime bondage. Only belief in God can free us from fear.

Doubts, anxiety, and insincerity play upon the dial of our prayer experiences, and discourage us greatly, so that it is not uncommon to hear it said: "I have prayed and prayed; I get no answer to my prayers; I don't see the use of praying any more." Again, faith must take the place of doubt, anxiety, and insincerity. It will doubtless be difficult to find the way there; but, on the way, watch for every indication of response; claim it as a scientist does in his findings. We must abandon the idea that God hears us for our much speaking. Never! But we will surely find Him in much seeking. We must examine both ourselves and our prayers, keeping before us always that God is examining with us, wants to give us the best, and is trying to establish between Him and us the highway of faith over which his answers go. The hindrance is within us. Only faith can remove hindrances—even mountains will remove before its breath (Matt. 17: 20).

HINDRANCES IN PRAYER

It must be said, too, that a divided and unreconciled Church can never so much as expect the power of prayer until its divisions are healed, and brotherhood of all Christians is a reality. Christ taught this both regarding individuals and the Church (Matt. 5:24; John 17). Paul regarded the divided Church as unspiritual and carnal (I Cor. 3:1-3). The present divisions of Christendom are unchristian and unnatural; they can only be abolished by genuine penitence in prayer.

However great may be our hindrances we can surmount them. We are made for it. We may be swayed by moods and held to certain courses by temperaments; but, when we make preparation,— and we have not tried at all if we have not some plan for the maintenance and development of our spiritual life,—we will find ourselves growing toward God. Sometimes it will seem to us that our prayers are but whispers to ourselves. We become discouraged, but we must keep on praying. Dean Goulburn says: "When you cannot pray as you would, pray as you can." Keep at it—not praying as others pray, but lifting up our souls to God as only we ourselves can do. It will be difficult to hold our mind on God, to make his interests first, to carry in our souls the reality of the communion, but the musician has had difficulty, too, in concentrating on perfect ideals. So has every one else who has tried to rise above the level of undeveloped possibilities. Writing in his diary, Benjamin Jowett

HINDRANCES IN PRAYER

says: " Nothing makes one more conscious of
poverty and shallowness of character than difficulty
in praying or attending to prayer. Any thoughts
about self, thoughts of evil, day-dreams, love
fancies, easily find an abode in the mind. But the
thought of God and of right and truth will not stay
there, except with a very few persons. I fail to
understand my own nature in this particular. There
is nothing which at a distance I seem to desire more
than the knowledge of God, the ideal, the universal;
and yet for two minutes I cannot keep my mind
upon them. But I read a great work of fiction, and
can hardly take my mind from it. If I had any real
love of God, would not my mind dwell upon Him? "

But the answer to that, which is our common
experience, lies in the power of the will to make its
choice. The heart may desire it, the mind may reason that it is wise; but, until the will identifies itself
freely with the will of God, there is no satisfactory
progress. Even then discouragement is common in
our experiences, due partly to our human weakness
and partly to our lack of knowledge of the processes
in the development of the human will, which is a
thing of growth and is designed to conform to the
will of God. This conformity is attained not by a
set of rules in morality, but rather by a real discovery of the Father's gracious will in dealing with
his children and, thereby, the will continues to function, moving unbribed from each discovery to larger
freedom. In spite of hindrances it continues to

choose God, who is forever seeking for us. "Wherever in all the world there is a human heart," says Alexander Whyte, " God also is there. And He is there in order to have that heart poured out before Him. And out of that, out of the aloneness of the human heart, and out of the nearness of God to every human heart, there immediately arises this supreme duty to every man who has a heart,—that he shall at all times pour his heart out before God. It is not the duty and privilege of psalmists and great saints only. It is every man's duty, and every man's privilege. And, indeed, all our duties to God are already summed up in this one great duty; and all our privileges are held out to us at once in this unspeakable privilege. ' Trust in Him at all times: ye people, pour out your heart before Him: God is a refuge for us.' " [1] Through many hindrances we hear his voice and make choice of Him, for we are made for Him and it is unnatural for us to be separated from Him.

---

[1] Alexander Whyte. *Lord, Teach Us to Pray* (Doran).

O Thou, Unseen and Eternal, by whose power we are upheld and by whose grace we are pardoned, have mercy on us. Take from us the sense of thy unreality, give us purity of heart and a forgiving attitude toward all, clear the dimness in our spiritual vision, command our temperaments, and let us not be discouraged because we have different ways of praying, nor be blind to thy gracious presence within us. Thou art wonderful in thy loving-kindness and we rejoice because thy search for us is always prior to any search that we have ever made for Thee. Bcause Thou hast found us Thou wilt fulfil thy promises in us and wilt lead us in the way to ever-lasting life that our fellowship with Thee may continue for ever and ever. Amen.

FATHER, I thank Thee for work and for the opportunity to work. I rejoice that in working I reflect some broken gleam of thy glory. Thou fillest the past and the present in all worlds with thy tireless energy, yet is there no fret or haste in all thy doing.

Grant that I also may do my appointed tasks with a sense of ease and mastery, always conscious that I am greater than they, and ever ready for still nobler efforts.

Save me from sullen discontent, from fruitless war with the circumstances of my lot. Make my heart obedient that by the untoward things of experience I may win a larger and freer life. Uphold me with the faith that Thou hast called me into fellowship with thy perfect Son who, when He dwelt among us, went about doing good.

In this faith be it mine to cheer the mourner, raise up the fallen, relieve the needy, forgive the wrong-doer, and praise the lover of simplicity and goodness. While I give to others, give Thou to me, that I may grow more and more in the spirit of helpfulness and generosity, both in word and deed. Amen.

—SAMUEL McCOMB (*Prayers for To-day—Harper*).

X

THE HURT OF HURRY IN PRAYER

NOTHING is more damaging to spiritual experience than hurry. Time and quiet are essential to worship. They are not choices, but are as necessary elements in spiritual growth as showers and mild weather are necessary for the revival of vegetation. Hurry in worship is like frost on flowers.

Where it has not taken away worship entirely, in many instances, and these are far too many, it has established short, and usually sloven, periods for Bible reading and prayer—just a few moments, so brief that there is no time for thought and meditation. Such practices are the sources of superficial piety, if not blight upon all spiritual growth.

Acquaintance with God can no more be hurriedly made than with an individual. In fact hurry, in either instance, rather indicates that acquaintance is not desired beyond mere selfish use. Consequently, hurried prayer ordinarily drops to the level of pagan worship. It is a question whether that kind of prayer is worth anything at all, with the overwhelming evidence against it as possessing any spiritual value.

Time is taken for eating, although sometimes that is shortened, but there is a tendency to linger around one of the meals, usually the evening meal.

THE HURT OF HURRY IN PRAYER

Time is taken for the newspaper. Time is taken for some pleasure, if only occasionally. There is time for work under heavy pressure through the day, and, perhaps, into the night. But nothing is needed in this world to-day more than time for prayer. We too frequently give everything else a place, but God, in whom we live and move and have our being. Not only is it proper to raise the question as to the wisdom of this course, but is it morally right?

If we enumerate the necessities of life, prayer belongs at the top of the list, because our spiritual natures are primary factors in our existence. The rush and hurry with which we are surrounded, and of which we unconsciously partake, contribute to the deadening of our spiritual experiences.

It is true the Lord's Prayer is brief and so are most of the prayers in the Bible, but those who prayed these short printed prayers, or gave them as suggestions as to how to pray, in some instances, as in that of Christ, " continued all night in prayer to God " (Luke 6: 12). Jacob wrestled all night and, therefore, we read " the God of Jacob is our refuge " (Psa. 46: 11). David prayed morning, noon, and night, and he became God's servant, whose " sure mercies " became the foundation of our everlasting covenant of redemption (Isa. 55: 3). In spite of the king's decree, Daniel kneeled before his open window toward Jerusalem, and prayed three times a day, and God gave him a vision of

THE HURT OF HURRY IN PRAYER

his Kingdom (Dan. 7: 1). Paul prayed continually
and exhorted the Christians to pray, saying: " Praying always with all prayer and supplication in the
Spirit, and watching thereunto with all perseverance and supplication for all saints " (Eph. 6: 18).
Long periods of prayer were the general practice of
the early Church.

In modern times we are reminded of Luther,
Wesley, Judson, Havelock, and others praying several hours a day. The practice of George Müeller
was to spend long periods with his open Bible on a
table before him, communing with God. Others
have used their Bibles, or special passages of Scripture, in thinking over their work to get God's point
of view in doing it. Bishop Moule's practice was a
standing attitude or walking up and down, either
indoors or out of doors. I have found for myself
both George Müeller's and Bishop Moule's plans
very satisfactory. After a period in such prayer,
one may be able to say with some confidence: " Lord
Jesus Christ, things stand between us on the old
terms," as Bengel was heard to say after working
for hours, late into the night, over his *Gnomon Novi
Testamenti*. The prayer itself need not be long,
but the communion with God should cover a lengthy
period if the prayer is to be effective. Some have
established horologic processes, so that at the striking of the clock there is a call to prayer—just a
brief upward thought. Men at the office, shop, or
factory; women about their household duties, enter-

taining friends, or at their place of business—any
one, anywhere can surely think for a moment of
God—if only an unspoken ejaculatory prayer.
Paul's exhortation is, "Pray without ceasing"
(I Thess. 5:17). Aristides, a first century Christian apologist, says in his *Apologia:* "Every morning and every hour Christians give thanks and praise
to God for his lovingkindness toward them; and
for their food and drink they offer thanksgiving to
Him."[1]

A suggestive horology may be as follows: 1 A. M.
—"When I remember Thee upon my bed, and meditate on Thee in the night watches" (Psa. 63:6).
2 A. M.—"I have remembered thy name, O Lord,
in the night, and have kept thy law" (Psa. 119:55).
3 A. M.—"In the morning, rising up a great while
before day, He went out, and departed into a solitary place, and there prayed" (Mark 1:35).
4 A. M.—"Jesus said unto him, Verily I say unto
thee, That this night, before the cock crow, thou
shalt deny me thrice" (Matt. 26:34). 5 A. M.—
"The morning stars sang together, and all the sons
of God shouted for joy" (Job 38:7). 6 A. M.—
"He maketh his sun to rise on the evil and the
good" (Matt. 5:45). 7 A. M.—"O come, let us
worship and bow down: let us kneel before the
Lord our Maker" (Psa. 95:6). 8 A. M.—"Whatsoever ye do, do it heartily, as to the Lord, and
not unto men" (Col. 3:23). 9 A. M.—Pouring out

[1] Aristides. *Apologia,* translation by Kay.

of the Holy Spirit, " for these are not drunken, as
ye suppose, seeing it is but the third hour of the
day " (Acts 2 : 15). 10 A. M.—" One is your Master, even Christ; and all ye are brethren " (Matt.
23 : 8). 11 A. M.—" Let the words of my mouth,
and the meditations of my heart, be acceptable in
thy sight, O Lord, my strength, and my redeemer "
(Psa. 19 : 14). 12 NOON—" When the sixth hour
was come, there was darkness over the whole land
until the ninth hour " (Mark 15 : 33). " Blotting
out the handwriting of ordinances that was against
us, which was contrary to us, and took it out of the
way, nailing it to his cross " (Col. 2 : 14). " Peter
went up upon the housetop to pray about the sixth
hour " (Acts 10 : 9). 1 P. M.—" Then enquired he
[the nobleman] of them the hour when he began
to amend. And they said unto him, Yesterday at
the seventh hour the fever left him " (John 4 : 52).
2 P. M.—" I, even I, am He that blotteth out thy
transgressions for mine own sake, and will not remember thy sins " (Isa. 43 : 25). 3 P. M.—" About
the ninth hour Jesus cried with a loud voice, saying,
Eli, Eli, lama sabachthani? that is to say, My God,
my God, why hast Thou forsaken Me? " (Matt.
27 : 46). " Peter and John went up together into
the temple at the hour of prayer, being the ninth
hour " (Acts 3 : 1). Cornelius " saw a vision evi-
dently about the ninth hour of the day " (Acts
10 : 3). 4 P. M.—James and John became disciples
of Jesus " and abode with Him that day : for it was

[85]

about the tenth hour" (John 1:39). 5 P. M.—
Calling for labourers in the Christian vineyard—
"And about the eleventh hour He went out, and
found others standing idle, and said unto them,
Why stand ye here all the day idle?" (Matt. 20:6).
6 P. M.—Christ abiding with the Emmaus disciples
—"And they constrained Him, saying, Abide with
us: for it is toward evening, and the day is far
spent. And He went in to tarry with them" (Luke
24:29). 7 P. M.—"Let my prayer be set forth before Thee as incense; and the lifting up of my
hands as the evening sacrifice" (Psa. 141:2).
8 P. M.—"Now when the even was come, He sat
down with the twelve. . . . And as they were
eating, Jesus took bread, and blessed it, and brake
it, and gave it to the disciples, and said, Take, eat;
this is my body. And He took the cup, and gave
thanks, and gave it to them, saying, Drink ye all
of it; for this is my blood of the new testament,
which is shed for many for the remission of sins"
(Matt. 26:20, 26–28). 9 P. M.—Christ blessing and
commissioning his Apostles—"At evening, being
the first day of the week, when the doors were shut
where the disciples were assembled for fear of the
Jews, came Jesus and stood in the midst, and saith
unto them, Peace be unto you" (John 20:19).

10 P. M.

> "The heavens declare the glory of God;
> And the firmament showeth his handiwork.
> Day unto day uttereth speech,
> And night unto night showeth knowledge"
>   (Psa. 19:1, 2).

THE HURT OF HURRY IN PRAYER

11 P. M.

> " Surely the darkness shall cover me;
> Even the night shall be light about me.
> Yea, the darkness hideth not from Thee;
> But the night shineth as the day;
> The darkness and the light are both alike to Thee"
> (Psa. 139: 11, 12).

12 MIDNIGHT—"At midnight I will rise to give thanks unto Thee because of thy righteous judgments" (Psa. 119: 62). The midnight struggle of Jesus in Gethsemane (Mark 14: 32–42). The parable of the midnight friend (Luke 11: 5–10). Paul and Silas prayed at midnight (Acts 16: 25). Jacob had his midnight prayer before he became Israel (Gen. 32: 24–28). "Behold, the bridegroom cometh!" (Matt. 25: 6) is the midnight cry. More than in any other hour, it appears that the midnight prayer has been winged with most courageous faith.

But time must be given to prayer. If necessary to find quiet, we should rise earlier or resort to some other practical plan that will satisfy our spiritual necessities. William Wilberforce says: "This perpetual hurry of business and company ruins me in soul if not in body. More solitude and earlier hours! I suspect I have been allotting habitually too little time to religious exercises, such as private devotion and religious meditation, Scripture reading, etc. Hence, I am lean and cold and hard. I had better allot two hours or an hour and a half daily. I have been keeping too late hours, and hence have had but a hurried half hour in a morning to myself. Surely the experience of all good men confirms the proposition that without a due measure of private devotions the soul will grow lean."

Our hurry may be in maintaining a method of Christian work. Then, it is still less inexcusable, for neither methods nor money nor culture can be a substitute for prayer. God's systems are men. These are the channels through which his grace flows. All enduring work must have foundations of prayer. Not even church activity can be a substitute for prayer. " To pray is the greatest thing we can do; and to do it well there must be calmness, time, and deliberation; otherwise it is degraded into the smallest and meanest of things." [1] There is nothing in life so urgent or important that we should lessen the time to pray. It is vital to us that we take time for communion and fellowship with God, who is revealed through Jesus Christ. To clear the vision to human eyes for a true understanding of Himself, God appeared in the person of his Son. It is the duty of faith to deal primarily with the reality of this revelation as it touches human life, going as far as Jesus seeks to take us, when He says: " Inasmuch as ye have done it unto one of the least of these my brethren, ye have done it unto Me " (Matt. 25:40). To do this it takes time for friendly observation, spiritual meditation, and the full appropriation of the Living Christ to our needs.

[1] E. M. Bounds. *Power Through Prayer* (Marshall).

O GOD OF PATIENCE AND PARDON, save us from the impoverishment and danger of hurry in our devotions, lest the bloom of our spiritual life be permanently blighted. Revive us from our leanness of soul and coldness of heart by awakening in us the sense of waiting and wrestling with Thee. Hush within us the first rise of murmurings against the taxing necessities of prayer. May there be no counting of the cost of time and labour, lest our foundations be imperiled. O Lord, pardon us of all slovenness in our devotions and set us to redeeming the time with gladness. Amen.

O Thou Great Companion of Our Souls, do Thou go with us to-day and comfort us by the sense of thy presence in the hours of spiritual isolation. Give us a single eye for duty. Guide us by the voice within. May we take heed of all the judgments of men and gather patiently whatever truth they hold, but teach us still to test them by the words and the spirit of the One who alone is our Master. May we not be so wholly of one mind with the life that now is that the world can fully approve us, but may we speak the higher truth and live the purer righteousness which Thou hast revealed to us. If men speak well of us, may we not be puffed up; if they slight us, may we not be cast down; remembering the words of our Master who bade us rejoice when men speak evil against us and tremble if all speak well, that so we may have evidence that we are still soldiers of God. Amen.

—Walter Rauschenbusch (*Prayers of the Social Awakening—Pilgrim Press*).

XI

THE DANGER OF BEING ALONE

SOLITUDE has its benefits. Great ideas have come out of it. The quiet hour is the summer of spirituality. It is necessary for spiritual growth. But there is no time in life so dangerous as when we are alone. The greatest temptations come at that time. No outward wrong has ever been done that has not been thought out, directly or indirectly, in solitude. This fact has been made clear in Bible history and present-day experience sustains it. The great temptation of Christ came when He was alone in the wilderness. We may put to flight the outward foe, and then be slain by our own thoughts when we retire to our room or stroll through the fields and forests.

The besetting sin is never so beseeching as then. Pride, retaliation, revenge, envy, jealousy, coveteousness, sensuality, and every other sin makes its approach at that time most attractively clothed. It invites our thoughts for a stroll down the path of imagination. There is no apparent harm, but the constant repetition establishes the besetting sin, always discovering the path which we are most willing to take—finding our weakest point; then, forever waiting there, and watching for every chance, when we are alone, for a stroll down the designated path. This continues until the thought is strong enough to break forth into an act.

We may have been wronged. Outwardly our conduct may be friendly. We may even say publicly kind things about the one who has wronged us. But, when alone, we think of retaliation, perhaps, revenge. We do not, of course, use those condemnatory terms, but our thoughts stroll down the path of imagination—perhaps this, perhaps that; and, perhaps, we are unconscious that we are strolling down a forbidden path until we feel the flush of resentment or of anger; even then we may continue in a self-conscious desire to set ourselves right, if only in our own eyes, and, perhaps, inflict wrong upon the one who has wronged us or whom we imagine has wronged us. A look or a word betrays the thought and, if the chance comes, retaliation or revenge takes a permanent place in our conduct. Then we have that awful word—unforgiveness.

It is unnatural for one to be constantly alone. Mankind is a fellowship. Unconsciously we are giving and receiving as we pass through the day. To make choice of solitude for study or prayer is one thing, keeping the mind steadily at the task; but it is quite another thing if the chosen solitude does not include God's presence. If the mind is allowed to roam at will through the day's transaction, or the transaction of some former days, recalling unholy

THE DANGER OF BEING ALONE

impressions, which are developed in solitude, one becomes unfit for the task of the succeeding day, and is violating the principle of living day by day.

In the soul's efforts to find a way out of present circumstances, which is a common experience, it may give itself to day dreaming, which, if only fantastic and unreal, may become detrimental, but, if any phase of unholiness is indulged in, it is hurtful to the soul. Spiritual guide-posts can be set up whenever we are alone. Thus, day dreaming may give way to spiritual imagination, which may take the soul into higher experiences. One must be on his guard that the period of solitude be used for spiritual advancement by the exercise of prayer.

We are likely to think of the crowded thoroughfares with their glitter and enticements as the most dangerous places. It is not so. They may have some danger, but the most dangerous temptations are when we are alone rather than when we are with people. Somehow the personal contact holds us to higher ideals. When we leave people, be they few or many, then is our danger. Impure actions always have back of them impure thoughts that are developed in the quiet. This is the interpretation of the Apostle Paul, when he exhorts to " put on the whole armour of God." It was not to meet the outward foe of " flesh and blood," but it was to rout " spiritual wickedness " that seeks the control of our thoughts and motives when we are alone. The inner wrestling is the severest in human experience. Then is the need of the whole armour, without which no one will be able to stand.

Others can help us in the crowd, but only God can help us when we are alone. If we will it so, the danger may be turned into opportunity for the lifting up of our souls to God in prayer. We need, therefore, to put on " the whole armour of God, that ye may be able to withstand in the evil day, and having done all, to stand " (Eph. 6:13). One of the functions of prayer is to light up the times that we are alone with the Living Presence for definite spiritual awakening. When Abraham was alone he heard God calling him, and God blessed him (Isa. 51:2). When Daniel was alone he saw the vision of God (Dan. 10:1-21). Christ frequently went alone to pray. Sometimes He prayed all night (Luke 6:12). Our being alone is an opportunity for prayer.

O THOU KEEPER OF MANKIND, leave us not when we go alone. Keep the human voice ringing in our ears and the remembrance of the human touch, however long we may be alone. O Thou tempted Son of God, come to us in the midst of our thoughts in order that we may be saved from hurting both thyself and us. We fear the strife of the open far less than the wrestling with our thoughts in our room or in the fields and forests. There Thou alone art the helper of the helpless. Put to shame our vanities, dispel our fears, and make our quiet hours aglow with thy Living Presence; through Jesus Christ our Lord. Amen.

'Tis God from heaven we hear,
As the Spirit listens near.
We hear his voice within us,
In tones of love most glorious.
Then like flick'ring candles burning,
Our thoughts waver in discerning,
Till from God comes gentle light,
Revealing in us sin's blight.
Such times noisy words are vain.
Thought meets thought in silent pain.
Curtained alone with Him and us,
It is his strong voice speaking thus,
" I will blot out all thy sin;
Gird thy strength to again begin."
To walk in truth's path anew
Adorns our best with golden hue.
'Tis done! Through wide gates of sense
Speaks love in fragrant incense.
Then all on earth and all above
Will know our hearts are bound in love.

XII

SILENT WORSHIP

A TYPE of prayer that is especially needed in these times of noise and rush, and that appeals strongly to certain temperaments, is silent worship. It has held a place in spiritual devotion throughout the history of religion. The Hebrews and early Christians give their witness to its worth. Later, striking instances are found among the Eastern Orthodox and Roman Catholics. Other instances are found, here and there, among various religious bodies. In the larger use of it by the Society of Friends—and no religious body has given such emphasis to it as the Friends—they show the rare fruits of it in a high standard of moral and spiritual life.

There is something about it that is wonderfully salutary in the soul's approach to God. It is a definite expression of obedience in the practice of self-retirement. "Enter into thy closet, and when thou hast shut thy door, pray to thy Father who is in secret" (Matt. 6:6). To retire within ourselves may be difficult to do, but self-retirement to some degree is a necessary part of all worship, especially of silent worship. God is everywhere; but, if we are able to expel from our thoughts the things that have crowded our minds through the day, and if we really take pains to retire within ourselves, we will find, in many instances, that the silence will create an atmosphere by which shall come into our souls the consciousness of the Living Presence.

It is a great privilege to pour out our needs to God, but it is a greater privilege to wait in silence for the impact of his Spirit upon ours. " Wait on the Lord: be of good courage, and He shall strengthen thine heart: wait, I say, on the Lord " (Psa. 27: 14). We are ever ready to ask for Divine guidance, but we too frequently hurry away before it is given, when, instead, we should be saying with the Psalmist: " I will hear what God the Lord will speak: for He will speak peace unto his people, and to his saints " (85: 8). Peace is never to be associated with a negative experience; it is always positive. It is the result of definite effort. It comes, perhaps, more deeply into life in periods of silence because the soul is then freer to receive spiritual impressions in its deeper self.

The impact of the Living Spirit upon our spirits is a method of God's approach to us. This must have been the experience of Amos, when he said: " The Lord God hath spoken, who can but prophesy? " (Amos 3: 8). While it is not the only method of God's approach to men, and is unsuited both in some instances and to some temperaments, nevertheless the method of spiritual impact runs through the experiences of Hebrew Prophets and

[98]

SILENT WORSHIP

Christian Apostles and Evangelists. It controlled Paul in his missionary tours, forbidding him to go in some instances, and directing him to go in other instances. It has been the experience of the great missionary pioneers. Multitudes of humble and unknown disciples bear witness to this leadership by the impact of the Living Spirit upon the human spirit.

The vital thing is the listening attitude. In silent worship we are not seeking for new thoughts; we are not concerned with things new or old; we are concerned only with Reality. " Speak, Lord; for thy servant heareth " (I Sam. 3 : 9). Most persons, who unreservedly open the door of their souls to God, will experience the true *sursum corda,* the lifting up of the soul into the Living Presence.

This silence may be for only a few moments, or it may continue for half an hour. It may precede a prayer or an address, or it may follow. It may begin with all saying the Lord's Prayer and close, in conformity with the custom of the Friends, by shaking hands; or it may begin with a Psalm and close with a Psalm, followed by the benediction. The meeting may be given a subject or it may be left free to find a subject.

But it must not be compulsory; it must not be allowed to become tiresome; its results must not be talked about afterward, whether satisfactory or unsatisfactory; its benefits must be discovered in our lives. It must be an experience in which the

soul has persevered into the Presence of the Living
Father, listening for his voice. "There was silence, and I heard a voice" (Job 4:16). "Be
silent, O all flesh, before the Lord; for He is raised
up out of his holy habitation" (Zech. 2:13).
"Truly my soul waiteth upon God; from Him
cometh my salvation" (Psa. 62:1). "Praise waiteth for Thee, O God, in Zion: and unto Thee shall
the vow be performed" (Psa. 65:1). As we enter
into the silence there must be a conscious surrender
of ourselves to God—penitence for unforgiveness,
revenge, envy, jealousy, sensuality, and all unrighteousness. "If I regard iniquity in my heart,
the Lord will not hear me" (Psa. 66:18). "If
we confess our sins, He is faithful and just to
forgive us our sins, and to cleanse us from all unrighteousness" (I John 1:9). Confession and
penitence are necessary if the soul would be free in
its fellowship with the Living Father, who is longsuffering and abundant in mercy to all who come
unto Him.

Before everything must be reverence, and such
reverence as establishes right relations with God.
It is a common thing to say that evil-doing is the
cause of delay in the coming of the Kingdom. As a
matter of fact, evil-doing is not the cause. The real
cause of delay is irreverence or sheer idolatry. The
world to-day is obsessed with a more insidious
idolatry than at any time in history. It has robbed
the Church of its spiritual power. No one follows

his own will except he is an idolater. The coming of the Kingdom means the rule of his will in us. There must first be reverence, then surrender, and then obedience. These form the trinity of the Christian's experience—all three perpetually functioning and making the heart able to receive Divine impressions and, likewise, to make impressions. Willing, waiting, and doing is the order.

The silence is a symbol of surrender. " Be still, and know that I am God " (Psa. 46: 10). Whatever may be our burdens or our needs, we must seek to bring our minds primarily to think of God— his goodness, his love, and his power. It may take longer to bring us to this than we anticipated, but the waiting and perseverance are worth while if we would find the listening attitude. In *The Fellowship of Silence* it is said: " It has to be remembered that this silent worship, dependent as it is on the attunement of many minds, is, in a way, a delicate instrument, more delicate than even the telephone or the telegraph, which transmits messages in the material world, and, therefore, easily jarred; yet it is even more certain and reliable, in its working, when faithfully used. Silence has perils of its own, just as speech has, but we find, in practice, that there are fewer perils in the two things used together than in either apart. To us, at any rate, compulsory silence is not healthy. To spend an hour in prearranged unbroken silence, where there is not liberty to speak, is like being shut up in a hothouse. True, there may be wonderful and beautiful plants all around us, exotic flowers, and fragrant scents, almost overpowering in their sweetness. It may be a wonderful experience to go through, now and then, but, to us at least, it would not be healthy to become dependent upon it, or to use it habitually. Such a silence is as different as possible from the free open-air atmosphere to which we are accustomed, with the wind of the Spirit sweeping over us and blowing where it listeth, as it does on a wide moor, or rippling over a barley field among the ears of living grain."[1] Silent worship has deepened the spiritual experience of many lives. It is a method of worship which needs to be given larger practice in the observance of the Lord's Supper, in Retreats, and in special meetings, as well as in one's private devotions. "I waited patiently for the Lord; and He inclined unto me, and heard my cry" (Psa. 40:1).

---

[1] L. A. Hodgkin. *The Fellowship of Silence* (Macmillan).

O GOD, Thou who hearest and Thou who speakest, from Thee cometh salvation. Because of thy still voice in the silence many have been revived in faith, hope, and love. There was no audible voice; it was a strange but natural impact of thy Spirit upon our spirits. Thy unspoken speech has been heard by thy listening servants through all the centuries of man's history. Rebuke our unwillingness to listen, and give us the consciousness of thy unspoken communion: then we shall be glad, when in the silence we have felt thy nearness and have called Thee Father; through Jesus Christ our Lord. Amen.

O MY FATHER, I have moments of deep unrest—moments when I know not what to ask by reason of the very excess of my wants. I have in these hours no words for Thee, no conscious prayers for Thee. My cry seems purely worldly; I want only the wings of a dove that I may flee away. Yet all the time Thou hast accepted my unrest as a prayer. Thou hast interpreted its cry for a dove's wings as a cry for Thee, Thou hast received the nameless longings of my heart as the intercessions of thy Spirit. They are not yet the intercessions of my spirit; I know not what I ask. But Thou knowest what I ask, O my God. Thou knowest the name of that need which lies beneath my speechless groan. Thou knowest that, because I am made in thine image, I can find rest only in what gives rest to Thee; therefore, Thou hast counted my unrest unto me for righteousness, and hast called my sighing thy Spirit's prayer. Amen.

—GEORGE MATHESON (*Great Souls at Prayer by Mary Tileston—Allenson*).

XIII

THE BIBLE AND PRAYER

THE Bible is the one prayer book of all history. On its pages may be found the earliest records of prayer, culminating in the Psalms, of which Ambrose says: " Those who listen to or read the Psalms aright, may find as if they had been written exclusively for themselves. Through them I learn to avoid sin, and unlearn being ashamed of repentance." The opening of the New Testament is made fragrant in the atmosphere of prayer; likewise, its close is marked by prayer; while through its pages walks Jesus Christ, the greatest interpreter of prayer.

The whole Bible is a small book. The New Testament may be read through in ten hours, and the Old Testament in three times ten. It is God's primer for mankind. We know it only when we practice it, as we know a rule in arithmetic, not when we can recite it, but when we are able to work the sum under that rule. For instance, quoting Scripture on forgiveness, and yet not trying to practice forgiveness, is evidence that we not only know little about the Scriptural principle of forgiveness, but we are, likewise, ignorant of the principles of prayer. It may be a lifetime task, and forgiveness is as hard a task in the lives of most individuals as the suppressing of any other sin, but not until one is able to work heroically at forgiveness can it be said that he understands either the Scriptures or prayer. It is so with every other principle. We may fail, and fail many times, but we must continue to work and pray courageously toward the ideal. Human life is just long enough to learn the principles of Divine living. A good rule in reading the four Gospels is to put ourselves in the place of every one with whom Jesus dealt. Just as soon as the person appears on the pages of the Gospel, let us put ourselves right in their place and hold that position throughout the narrative. If we are not just that person, we might have been. To all Christ is Friend and Redeemer.

The Psalms afford the finest expressions of the soul's need to be found anywhere. Athanasius says: " In this book thou findest the whole life of man pictured, the moods of the heart, the movements of the thoughts. If thou hast need of repentance, if thou hast met trial and temptation, if thou art exposed to persecution and calumny, in all and in every case, thou canst find here instruction, and bring thy case before God in the words of the Psalms."

In this little volume may be found some of the most choice Psalms, classified as follows: (1) Penitential—6th, 32nd, 38th, 39th, 51st, 102nd, 130th, and 143rd. (2) Thanksgiving—30th, 46th, 65th,

THE BIBLE AND PRAYER

66th, 67th, 96th, 107th, 116th, 124th, and 138th.
(3) Petition—25th, 41st, 43rd, 63rd, 86th, 119th
(33-40), 123rd, 141st, and 142nd. (4) Nature—
8th, 19th, 29th, 93rd and 104th. (5) Adoration—
103rd, 111th, 145th, 146th, 147th, 148th, and 150th.
These, and others, may be read and reread with
most salutary results, especially if we are in the
mood of penitence, of spiritual fellowship, and
courage, or of thanksgiving, or of petition, or of
nature, or of adoration. We may sweep through
the whole Bible and, everywhere, prayer is a
reality in the lives of those who pray. Hence,
above all books, the Bible should be read until
our reading becomes prayer. Read it over and
over. Its lessons are difficult to learn. In many
instances we are put to shame because of the indifference with which we go to prayer and the little
value we put on the petition we make.

The prayers of the Bible are the expressions of
living speech. Paul's prayers in Ephesians and
Colossians are superb instances. Austin Phelps
says: " Let a man approach God with both vague-
ness of thought and languor of emotion; and what
else can his prayer be, but a weariness to himself
and an abomination to God? It would be a miracle,
if such a suppliant should enjoy success in prayer.
He cannot succeed, he cannot have joy, because he
has no *object* that elicits intense desire, and no *desire* that sharpens his object. He has no great,
holy, penetrative thought in him, which stirs up

his sensibilities; and no deep, swelling sensibility, therefore, to *relieve* by prayer. His soul is not reached by anything he is thinking about, and, therefore, he *has* no soul to pour out before God. Such a man prays because he thinks he *must* pray; not because he is grateful to God that he *may* pray. There is an unspeakable difference between 'must' and 'may.' It is his conscience that prays; it is not his heart. His language is the language of his conscience. He prays in words which ought to express his heart, not in those which do express it."[1]

The weakness of prayer is the lack of faith. Writing to the Roman Christians Paul affirms that faith comes by hearing the word of God (Rom. 10:17). Where there is the slightest doubt, we must not hesitate to bring to bear the severest proof. Both the Old and New Testaments invite investigation (Mal. 3:10; John 1:39). In simplifying difficult passages it will be helpful to make use of the various versions, such as the Revised, the American Revised, Weymouth's, Moffatt's, Riverside, and others. We must not be afraid of the findings of scholarship. The Bible is a book of growth. Its various books and letters were not combined into one volume, as we now have it, until the fourth century of our Christian era. But scholarship is not enough. It must be put into human experience. In this we must be no less

[1] Austin Phelps. *The Still Hour* (Lothrop, Lee & Shepard Co.).

THE BIBLE AND PRAYER

severe in dealing with our experience than scholars are in dealing with the text. We must find reality whatever it may cost us.

In our study of the Bible it must ever be kept in mind that it is a book dealing with righteousness, interpreting Divine standards of motive, disposition, and conduct as related to mankind. Without argument its open pages reveal in the simplest style man's possibility of spiritual achievement. In fact, it marks out unerringly his normal path, showing all other paths to be abnormal, and leaves for contemplation the most fascinating dream that ever captivated a human soul.

It does not argue for prayer. It assumes that prayer is the normal state between God and man, as natural as the wind, or the waves, or flying birds, or growing plants. It is a part of man's existence, more vital to the complete man than any one of his five senses, or all of his five senses combined. Prayer uses the senses as roads over which to travel and in the practice of prayer wide visioned men speak in the name of God. John Ruskin says that, in his childhood, two or three chapters from the Bible were read to him every day by his mother, who required him to commit certain passages every day to memory and that he thus learned, and was able to recite, the following portions of Scripture: Exodus 15th and 16th chapters, II Samuel 1:17–27, I Kings 8th chapter, Psalms 23rd, 32nd, 90th, 91st, 103rd, 112th, 119th, and 139th, Proverbs 2nd,

3rd, 8th, and 12th chapters, Isaiah 53rd chapter, Matthew 5th, 6th, and 7th chapters, Acts 26th chapter, I Corinthians 13th and 15th chapters, James 4th chapter, and Revelation 5th and 6th chapters. In after years he wrote: " I consider this the most precious and, on the whole, the one essential part of my education."

The Scriptural examples of prayer are direct and intense. We think of the wrestling of Jacob and hear him say: " I will not let thee go, except thou bless me " (Gen. 32: 26) ; and the cry of Bartimæus: " Have mercy on me " (Mark 10: 48) ; Christ Himself saying: " If it be possible ——" (Matt. 26: 39) ; and that great Scriptural exhortation, for ever calling us to prayer: " Let us come boldly unto the throne of grace, that we may obtain mercy, and find grace to help in time of need " (Heb. 4: 16). Each of us must come face to face with the Word of God itself. This is the purpose of the written word, but God is forever writing—writing living epistles in the hearts of all who pray.

O Thou Holy One, before whom is loving-kindness and truth, cause thy face to shine upon us. We acknowledge our sins and bless Thee because Thou hast put away our sins. Search us; try us; lead us by thy light; set a watch at the door of our lips, and teach us the art of laying up thy word in our hearts. Amid the din and fascination of this fading world, our eyes look unto Thee, for we prefer Thee above all else, and our chief desire is to possess thy beauty. Receive our prayer as the incense of this holy worship between Thee and us and make our souls harps upon which only thy · fingers shall play. Let all that is within us adore Thee for ever and ever, for unto Thee belong praise and dominion and glory for ever. Amen.

THOU art ever patient with me, as a father with the unfulfilled promise of his child. I am dear to Thee, not mainly for the little that I do aright; but for my penitence after doing wrong; for my desire to do better; for what in due time with thy help I shall become.

Help me to keep this humility I learn from Thee in my attitude toward my fellow men. May I never try to pass with them as better than Thou seest me to be. May I esteem them better than myself; having reverence and tenderness for all; pride and uncharitableness toward none.

When enemies and censorious critics detect me in some fault, and try to break me down; then may the humility I have learned from Thee become my armour and defense. Knowing how light are their worst charges in comparison to what Thou knowest against me, and in spite of knowing still forgivest, still lovest; may I be strong in the confidence that no weakness acknowledged, no fault confessed, no mistake corrected no sin repented, can ever separate me from Thee, or from the friends Thou givest to all who walk in true humility. Amen.

—WILLIAM DE WITT HYDE (*Abba Father—Revell*).

XIV

TEMPTATION AND PRAYER

PRAYER is forever associated with temptation. Human life is a warfare. It begins with the first cry of the infant and ends with the last sigh at the gate of death. Between these two extremes, human life is made. In this process of making, the best made life is that in which prayer has been the contending factor in the midst of the things that defile us. " From within, from the heart of man, the designs of evil come: sexual vice, stealing, murder, adultery, lust, malice, deceit, sensuality, envying, slander, arrogance, recklessness, all these evils issue from within and they defile a man " (Mark 7: 21–23).[1] We cannot conquer by our own strength. We have tried it often and have failed just as often. But by prayer Divine power is brought into the struggle. Even then, we fail and become discouraged until the very roots within us are pulled up, and gradually, step by step, through patience and courage, the soul is again free. " For it is God, who worketh in you both to will and to do of his good pleasure " (Phil. 2: 13).

The frontiers of temptation, however severely enticing they may be, do not hurt us; it is when we

---

[1] Moffatt's Translation.

pass the frontiers and go into the temptation itself that we become spiritually wounded. Thomas à Kempis says: " The beginning of all temptation to evil is instability of temper and want of trust of God; for even as a ship without a helm is tossed about by the waves, so is a man who is careless and infirm of purpose tempted, now on this side, now on that. As fire testeth iron, so doth temptation the upright man. Oftentimes we know not what strength we have; but temptation revealeth to us what we are. Nevertheless, we must watch, especially in the beginnings of temptation; for then is the foe the more easily mastered, when he is not suffered to enter within the mind, but is met outside the door as soon as he hath knocked. Wherefore one saith:

> Check the beginnings; once thou might'st have cured,
> But now 'tis past thy skill, too long hath it endured.

For first cometh to the mind the simple suggestion, then the strong imagination, afterward pleasure, evil affection, assent. And so, little by little, the enemy entereth in altogether, because he was not resisted at the beginning. And the longer a man delayeth his resistance, the weaker he groweth, and the stronger groweth the enemy against him." [1]

The common weapon in temptation is ejaculatory prayer—just a single petition, calling for help. Perhaps, there are more prayers of this character

---

[1] Thomas à Kempis. *The Imitation of Christ.*

than any other. It may be when we are with others
or alone; but, when the habit of ejaculatory prayer
is established in our lives we have gone a long way
toward putting round about ourselves the defenses
of God, who is our refuge at all times; likewise use
the great hymns. They are powerful appeals to
spirituality.

No one is free from temptation. Some have their
severest struggle at the beginning of the Christian
life; others, after being in the Christian life for
many years; others have theirs at the end; and still
others have a whole lifetime of struggle. Some
have one weakness, some another; but all have a
weak place where the foe enters. Some of us fail
and fail wretchedly, others of us fail and try again.
Through temptation we are taught, proved,
humbled, and purified. We would not want to be
without it, if we could. Not only is there an open
door for our escape from every temptation, but God
is always with us in the struggle. " There hath no
temptation taken you but such as is common to
man; but God is faithful, who will not suffer you
to be tempted above that ye are able; but will with
the temptation also make a way to escape, that ye
may be able to bear it " (I Cor. 10: 13).

We too frequently hold to our threadbare notions
of Adam as being the normal man; he was not.
The normal man is Christ. Through Him God has
revealed our possibilities, leaving us a pattern of
life that is the hope of the world. Rufus M. Jones

says: " Christianity is essentially, I should say, a unique revelation of God. Here for the first time the race discovers that God identifies Himself with humanity, is in the stream of it, is suffering with us, is in mortal conflict with sin and evil, is conquering through the travail and tragedy of finite persons, and is eternally, in mind and heart and will, a God of triumphing Love. No texts adequately ' prove ' this mighty truth. We cannot tie it down to ' sayings,' though there are ' sayings ' which declare it. The life of Jesus, the supreme decisions through which He expresses his purpose, the spirit which dominates Him and guides his decisive actions, make the truth plain that God meant *that* to Him and that his way of life revealed that kind of God."[1]

When we get this understanding of temptation we feel the challenge within us to holier living. James was so thrilled by it that he opened his epistle, exclaiming, " My brethren, count it all joy when ye fall into divers temptations " (Jas. 1:2). Likewise, Peter, in his first epistle, says: " Beloved, think it not strange concerning the fiery trial which is to try you, as though some strange thing happened unto you: but rejoice. inasmuch as ye are partakers of Christ's sufferings; that, when his glory shall be revealed, ye may be glad also with exceeding joy " (I Pet. 4:12, 13). There is nothing in the wide

---

[1] Rufus M. Jones. *Spiritual Energies in Daily Life* (Macmillan).

range of human experience that furnishes a parallel to the spiritual magnificence of the struggle in temptation, except the matchless life of Christ. He found his power of resistance in prayer. In his last great struggle—the struggle in the garden—He said to his disciples: " Watch ye and pray, lest ye enter into temptation " (Mark 14: 38). This is our only safety. Beset as we are with foes behind and before, arrayed in spiritual warfare, we must venture into the experiences of the reality of God, not trusting to ourselves, but to Him, who neither failed nor was discouraged.

———

O GOD, Thou guide of the humble, give us the spirit of wisdom that we may be saved from false choices. Lead us to walk humbly with Thee in the path of justice and mercy. Grant we beseech Thee that Christ may be formed in us and thereby all manner of sin be cast out of our hearts. In the midst of temptation give us courage to contend, and, if we falter, give us good sight that we may see the open door of escape, for except we are upheld by Thee we shall strive in vain for the crown of life which Thou hast prepared for them that love Thee. Scatter our sins as the morning clouds and let thy Holy Spirit so possess us that we may keep thy commandments unto the end; through Jesus Christ our Lord. Amen.

O Lord, give thy blessing, we pray Thee, to our daily work, that we may do it in faith and heartily, as to the Lord and not unto men. All our powers of body and mind are thine, and we would fain devote them to thy service. Sanctify them, and the work in which they are engaged; let us not be slothful, but fervent in spirit, and do Thou, O Lord, so bless our efforts that they may bring forth in us the fruits of true wisdom. Teach us to seek after truth and enable us to gain it; but grant that we may ever speak the truth in love; that, while we know earthly things, we may know Thee, and be known by Thee, through and in thy Son Jesus Christ. Give us this day thy Holy Spirit, that we may be thine in body and spirit in all our work and all our refreshments: through Jesus Christ thy Son, our Lord. Amen.

—THOMAS ARNOLD (*Great Souls at Prayer by Mary W. Tileston—Allenson*).

XV

COMMON DUTIES AND PRAYER

THERE is no place in life where we so easily lose the sense of the consciousness of God as in the performance of our daily duties. If we keep the Morning Watch, we think of Him as there; if we attend public worship, we think of Him as there; and, if we go through the forests or walk on the ocean beach, especially if alone, we can easily think of God as there; but, when we go to the routine of daily duties,—the office, the shop, the factory, the court room, the classroom, the store, the market, the kitchen, or any other fields of household and business obligations,— our conscious mind is so occupied that it is difficult to conceive of God as even interested in the daily routine of our little, individual lives.

But He is. Not a sparrow falls to the ground, nor does a blade of grass wither, without his notice. There is nothing too small in our lives but has the interest of God—the opening of a letter, the entering of an account, the placing of a bolt, the purchase of an article, the laying of a brick, the opening of a book, the washing of a dish, or the greeting of an individual. By the practice of excluding God from the routine of daily duties, He becomes unreal to us, and our neglect of Him proves disastrous to us. Spiritual values are easily forgot amid the rush and bustle of daily routine. The simplicity of Christianity lies in the task of daily duties. It is in this field we learn to forgive our enemies, to practice self-denial, to deal justly, to control our temper, to be kind to the needy, and to walk humbly with God. However virtuous and honourable we may appear when we are through with our daily routine, that virtue and honour are not ours unless they are practiced in the midst of the daily routine. Consciousness of God belongs at the counter for correct business as much as a customer for doing business. The practice of the presence of God is wonderfully emphasized in the little book of that title by Brother Lawrence.[1]

The prayer attitude may be taken with us into every kind of task, however difficult and vexing it may be, and it will make possible our adjustment to unpleasant circumstances. These are the experiences that interpret to us the new birth, the cross-bearing, the surrendered life, and the everlasting hope. Paul reminds us that all work is primarily to God (Col. 3 : 23) and that practice of prayer is a continual experience (Col. 4 : 2). Wrongs are to be adjusted in the light of these facts. God is just, and his justice must be seen in

---

[1] Brother Lawrence. *The Practice of the Presence of God.*

the attitudes of capital and labour, of employer and employee, and in the comradeship of team work.

Public worship has its value, but emphasis here, which is on the spiritual values that must find outlets of expression in the common duties of daily life, is of far more consequence than emphasis on public worship. William Law says: " It is very observable, that there is not one command in all the Gospel for public worship; and perhaps it is a duty that is least insisted upon in Scripture of any other. The frequent attendance at it is never so much as mentioned in all the New Testament. Whereas that religion or devotion which is to govern the *ordinary actions* of our life, is to be found in almost every verse of Scripture. Our blessed Saviour and his Apostles are wholly taken up in doctrines that relate to *common life.* They call us to renounce the world, and differ in every *temper* and *way* of life, from the spirit and way of the world—to renounce all its goods, to fear none of its evils, to reject its joys, and have no value for its happiness; to be as new *born babes,* that are born into a new state of things, to live as *pilgrims* in spiritual watching, in holy fear, and heavenly aspiring after another life; to take up our daily cross, to deny ourselves, to profess the blessedness of mourning, to seek the blessedness of poverty of spirit; to forsake the pride and vanity of riches, to take no thought for the morrow, to live in the profoundest state of humility, to rejoice in worldly sufferings; to reject the lust of the flesh, the lust of the eyes, and the pride of life; to bear injuries, to forgive and bless our enemies, and to love mankind as God loveth them; to give up our whole hearts and affections to God, and strive to enter through the straight gate into a life of eternal glory.

" This is the *common devotion* which our blessed Saviour taught, in order to make it the *common life* of all Christians. Is it not, therefore, exceeding strange, that people should place so much piety in the attendance upon public worship, concerning which there is not one precept of our Lord's to be found, and yet neglect these common duties of our *ordinary life,* which are commanded in every page of the Gospel? I call these duties the devotion of our *common life,* because if they are practiced, they must be made parts of our common life; they can have no place anywhere else." [1]

The change of the world lies not so much in the conduct of people at public worship on Sunday, as in the conduct of people in common duties of every-day life. The reason why the world has not changed more since the advent of Christianity is because the prayer attitude has not had a place in our common duties. If the whole Church were to adopt the practice of real prayer, schism would forthwith be healed and racial animosities would be removed; likewise, if Christians in all nations would give

---

[1] William Law. *A Serious Call.*

themselves to the practice of real prayer, war would forthwith be abolished and proper industrial relations would be established between employer and employee. None of these things will attain to permanency apart from real prayer. Prayer is the way. Instances are found here and there where this attitude has been maintained, but multitudes of Christians live just like people who are not Christians—not immoral, profane, or intemperate, but possessing the same temper, the same attitude, and seeking the same end. Nothing can change this condition but prayer. The common duties of life are the shrines where prayer is to transform work and workers until we become conscious of the Living Presence and possess abounding joy.

———

O GOD, our Father, gracious and merciful, give us such vision of the duties of our common life that we may see in them altars of daily sacraments where our souls may become lamps, refilled and illuminated by Thee. Lead us into the experiences of humility, self-denial, renunciation of the world, consciousness of spiritual need, and heavenly affection, in order to overcome worldly temper, sensual pleasures, and the pride of life. Plant in us thy Spirit that we may see the beauties of our common life and interpret them in a godly walk with our fellows; through Jesus Christ our Lord. Amen.

FORTIFY my soul, blessed Jesus, with the same spirit of submission with which Thou underwentest the death of the Cross, that I may receive all events with resignation to the will of God; that I may receive troubles, afflictions, disappointments, sickness, and death itself, without amazement. Let this be the constant practice of my life, to be pleased with all thy choices, that when sickness and death approach, I may be prepared to submit my will to the will of my Maker. And O that, in the meantime, my heart may always go along with my lips in this petition—thy will be done. Amen.

—BISHOP WILSON (*Sacra Privata—Methuen*).

XVI

THE MINISTRY OF HEALING

THE world throbs with pain. It is the common experience of mankind, irrespective of nationality or class. Scientific attempts have been made through the centuries to alleviate it; likewise, healing cults have multiplied around the world. That both science and the healing cults have cures to their credit is heartily recognized. The greatest physician, however, is Christ. He outdistanced all healers and stands alone as the only healer before whom all diseases cowered.

While many are clamouring to heal the sick as Christ did, it is well to remember that there are many things in the life of Christ to be possessed by us of far more importance than healing the sick. It was not primary in his ministry. John the Baptist was the greatest of all prophets, but he did not heal the sick; neither does it appear that Christ selected his Apostles from any of those whom He cured, and, according to Scriptural records, those whom Christ cured passed out of sight, so far as value of service to Him was concerned. But Christ did heal the sick, and his healing was based upon the fact of Himself.

THE MINISTRY OF HEALING

Because of who He is, his cures are altogether possible and probable. To deny either the physical or moral possibility, or their probability, makes God unfree. But God is a free Spirit, immanent and transcendent, and, therefore, He is not bound to certain limitations, as men count limitations. The coming of Christ among men was a sufficient occasion for the working of cures upon a race to whom God sought to reveal Himself as God and Father. The physical possibility of the cures of Christ could rest simply upon the absolute and immutable will of God, but immutability must not be confused with rigidity and fixedness. The steadiness of God's unchangeable purpose includes, and even requires variety, in execution. The healings wrought by Christ furnish one of these varieties.

It is, likewise, so morally. A thing may be physically possible, but not morally possible. In the instance of the healings wrought by Christ, they are morally possible because the moral attributes of God are holiness and love. We could not think of God except in these terms. However these terms— holiness and love—may be defined, there must be a general agreement that any definition of them would include God's gift of Himself to his creatures. Consequently, moved by the holiness and the love of God, the will of God worked in Christ for the healing of the sick.

Also, the healings wrought by Christ possess a large degree of antecedent probability expressed in

the five great words—" providence," " revelation,"
" prayer," " redemption," and " fellowship." These
words stand for pathways over which God and
man have had communion. They interpret the
mightiest experiences of the human soul. God's
providence was the beginning of man's history, or
there would have been no history of man for which
to have a beginning. It is, likewise, so of revelation.
Both his providence and his revelation have been
approved through all ages. A multitude of altars
crowd the world. They are the places of prayer.
The spirit of prayer comes from God and that
spirit presses for entrance upon our souls. It is
not that our prayers are changing God, but God is
so changing us that we are finding in his will the
highest joy of human experience. " Prayer," says
Brierley, " is the gracious circulating of Divine ideas
through the human soul." Prayer brings us to
want what God wants us to have. This easily
breaks through the mechanical theory that the universe is a closed system. It means that God is
entering into personal converse with man, and that
man is answering back. Both redemption and fellowship are antecedently probable and morally necessary in order that God should make Himself
known to his creatures as Lord and Saviour. With
this rich background of human experience the healings wrought by Jesus are antecedently probable as
recorded in the Scriptures.

In this brief survey of the possibility and probability of the healings wrought by Christ, it is shown that his cures stand apart from all others, as He stands apart from all other healers, saying to us, as He said to the disciples of John the Baptist: " The blind receive their sight, and the lame walk, the lepers are cleansed, and the deaf hear, the dead are raised up, and the poor have the Gospel preached to them. And blessed is he, whosoever shall not be offended in me " (Matt. 11 : 5, 6).

Many, if not most, diseases are mental. They are frequently stubborn and sometimes become so serious as to prove fatal. In these fields the healing cults appear to have largely got their results, and in saying this, it is no discredit to them, but only to indicate their field of operation. It is difficult to make a definite classification as to which diseases are, and which are not, affected by suggestion. We are, at once, involved in two great unsolved mysteries. The first has to do with the relation of thought to the brain, and the second has to do with the processes of suggestion. We know that the mind affects the body and that the body, in turn, affects the mind. They are interdependent with pathways abounding in mystery. Suggestion to the subconscious mind appears to be more powerful if neither the attendant nor the patient is working to secure it. It is established in one instance and fails of establishment in another. If confidence can supplant fear, a long step has been made toward recovery. Religious motives furnish the most powerful appeal, especially to one who is sick, and the healing is frequently attended with most fruitful results as to future physical health and spiritual experience. All of this has therapeutic value which merits commendation in a world where sin and disease are so common. Prayer and faith have wrought results in religious experience, which have given calmness and confidence to the subconscious mind, stimulating the activities of mental health, which profoundly affects the state of the body.

But where there is a broken bone or bone trouble or a dangerous fever or some similar disease, science must minister through skilled surgeons and skilled physicians, and it has ministered in amazing satisfaction to the cures of multitudes. Surgeons have fought great battles over the operating table, as physicians have in the sick room. Pain has been wonderfully alleviated and multitudes have been snatched from the jaws of death, and given health where health had been despaired of. If the Apostle Paul could call the civil officer " a minister of God to thee for good," how much more " the beloved physician " should be called a minister of God to you for health? The service of the physician and surgeon is sacred, and is preëminently the work of God, whether science recognizes it or not. It is one of the fields in which God is training men in kindness for service to their fellows. Sir Oliver Lodge says: " You might almost as well try to cure disease by prayer without treatment, as to try to cure it by treatment without prayer. You must use both."

The surgeon or physician, however, who ignores all spiritual help in his practice belongs in the class of those healing cults that ignores material help for all diseases. Multitudes of Christian physicians and surgeons, however, take their patients to God in prayer. One of the greatest defects in the educational training of the physician and surgeon is the too frequent absence of the spiritual. So manifest is this that it is not infrequent that young men, spiritually inclined at the beginning of their educational course, are anything else but spiritual at the close. Some of the most successful physicians and surgeons are as forgetful of God's part in their healings, as irreligious farmers are of God's part in their farming. Neither stops to give God thanks. Herein lies the goodness and greatness of God. He gives to all his love and care. "He maketh his sun to rise on the evil and on the good, and sendeth rain on the just and on the unjust" (Matt. 5:45).

However widely we may differ about these matters, we cannot escape the conclusion that healing the sick is a part of the ministry of the Church—not only in providing hospitals and sanitariums and physicians and surgeons and nurses, but sometimes when there are none of these, just as God's grace is not confined to the Church, but righteousness may spring forth where there is no Church. God is not limited, however definitely we may be. There

THE MINISTRY OF HEALING

was but little science in medicine and surgery in the days of the Apostles, and that little was very crude; consequently, prayer functioned in healing independent of their help. But because these sciences have developed and have been a blessing to mankind, that is no reason that prayer should be excluded, either from the sick room with physicians and surgeons or, in some instances, where there are neither physicians nor surgeons.

We cannot think of God as the loving Father in any other terms than his desire for the health and happiness of all mankind. He, likewise, desires that we shall have the comforts of life—not that one shall grab and get so much of this world's possessions as to deprive others of equal comforts, but that all may have every need supplied. Just as the world is abnormal in comforts,—some having and others not having,—so it is in health—some are healthy and others are always in the grip of disease. By the help of God, we are to go to the root of both evils, contending for the right of every man to have a chance and, likewise, seeking health for all mankind.

Immediately following the day of Pentecost, the ministry of healing was practiced throughout the Apostolic age (Acts 3: 1–16; 5: 15, 16; 8: 6, 7; 9: 32–41; 14: 8–10; 16: 16–18, etc.). It was affirmed then that the prayer of faith saved the sick, and James advised the combining of prayer with the ordinary medical treatment of oil (Jas. 5: 14–16).

THE MINISTRY OF HEALING

We may use drugs, surgery, diet, manipulations, psychical methods, or devotional and sacramental means; but, in all of these, faith may, and often does, create powerfully in the patient a disposition toward health. Just as we are trying to learn how to live spiritually, we must, likewise, learn to live biologically. To do either or both we must be instructed. Hence, preventive measures in both spirituality and biology hold priority over cures. However, in the presence of disease faith is a great factor. On one occasion the Apostles were unable to heal for the lack of it (Matt. 17:21). Perhaps, we need a ministry of pain or mortification, such as a thorn in the flesh as Paul had—blindness, epilepsy, malaria,[1] or some painful disease—in order to know the abundant grace of God. "My grace is sufficient for thee: for my strength is made perfect in weakness" (II Cor. 12:9). But whatever our explanations may be, prayers for the sick, whether they be absent or present, are a part of the ministry of the Church. To come before God for such a cause, there must be penitence of heart, humility of spirit, and all absence of self-interest. If it be talked about, as the work of some individual, the transaction is ruined. "He that glorieth, let him glory in the Lord" (I Cor. 1:31).

---

[1] Some conclude it was a defective sight in consequence of Gal. 6:11; Lightfoot suggested epilepsy and Ramsay suggested malaria.

THE MINISTRY OF HEALING

Out of such an experience the healing may come, or for some reason, it may not come. " If we ask any thing according to his will, He heareth us " (I John 5 : 14). In the great prayer of Christ before his crucifixion, He said: " Not my will, but thine, be done " (Luke 22 : 42). The triumph of the will of God in Christ is a greater fact than his crucifixion on the cross. So it must be in our sickness. Nevertheless, there are instances where prayer may function in free conformity to the promise of our Lord: " Verily, verily, I say unto you, He that believeth on me, the works that I do shall he do also; and greater works than these shall he do; because I go unto my Father " (John 14 : 12).

O THOU GREAT PHYSICIAN, heal us in soul and body. Bless all physicians, surgeons, nurses, hospitals, and sanitariums; but let us never forget that before these were Thou didst heal the sick and bless mankind with health. Grant us wisdom to combine what these have found for our health and give to them the benediction of prayer; likewise, O Lord, help us to possess the courage of faith that will not stagger at thy promises, but ask direct for healing power. If it be thy will that we carry a thorn in the flesh, make thy grace be sufficient for us and, when we come to leave the body, make our home going as natural as tides go out to the sea; through Jesus Christ our Lord. Amen.

I WILL bless the Lord at all times: his praise shall continually be in my mouth.

My soul shall make her boast in the Lord: the humble shall hear thereof, and be glad.

O magnify the Lord with me, and let us exalt his name together.

I sought the Lord, and He heard me, and delivered me from all my fears.

They looked upon Him, and were lightened: and their faces were not ashamed.

This poor man cried, and the Lord heard him, and saved him out of all his troubles.

The angel of the Lord encampeth round about them that fear Him, and delivereth them.

—Psalm 34: 1-7.

XVII

A RETREAT

A METHOD that has been used for many centuries as a powerful and practical help toward a more complete surrender to Christ is withdrawing for a day, or perhaps for several days, for meditation, self-examination, and prayer. It may be at some regular time or occasionally. Thomas Chalmers, of Scotland, made it a practice once a month to go apart for a whole day; others have had similar practices. Annual retreats, especially when the groups are made up of persons from many communions, are attended with great blessing, if they are taken seriously and entered into courageously. It is a time of drawing near to God. In the opening of a retreat, such passages of Scripture as the sixth chapter of Isaiah and the fifth chapter of Revelation may be read.

However a retreat may be conducted, the chief elements are meditation, self-examination, and prayer. It is work, as is all real prayer. It is both humiliating and refreshing: humiliating, because it is the supplication of one who is conscious of his weakness and helplessness,—" Have mercy upon me, O God, according to thy lovingkindness: according unto the multitude of thy tender mercies blot out my transgressions " (Psa. 51 : 1),—and refreshing, because God satisfies all who come humbly unto Him—" As the hart panteth after the water brooks, so panteth my soul after Thee " (Psa. 42 : 1). It is, likewise, courageous. A retreat means self-examination—a sincere and thorough observation of oneself in the consciousness that Christ is observing with us. A definite time set apart for such experience contributes to health of soul.

Whenever the time may be, it should be when the mind is alert and ready for some fresh task. The address or addresses should be brief and suggestive of closer fellowship with Christ. Much time should be given to silent worship. From the beginning to the close a retreat should have about it the atmosphere of real prayer, with a definite perseverance toward the Living Presence for that peace that passes all understanding (Phil. 4 : 7). We should always go immediately from a retreat to our task.

There are certain guide-posts in a retreat, especially when a retreat covers several days, that should have consideration. These may be enumerated as follows :

(1) Thoughts on God as our heavenly Father. " This is life eternal, that they might know Thee the only true God, and Jesus Christ, whom Thou hast sent " (John 17 : 3). God is the basis of our experience. After defining and combining his at-

tributes, all definitions and combinations break
down, for God is greater than the sum of all his
attributes. "Holy and reverend is his name"
(Psa. 111:9). In our meditations we must examine ourselves as to our attitude of reverence,
both toward God and toward all mankind, irrespective of races or classes; likewise, reverence for
ourselves, for we are his workmanship (Eph.
2:10). Humour is healthy, but it must not drop
to the level of the obscene or be used irreverently
of God and mankind, neither should we make one
of God's children the subject of constant satire.
We must practice reverence.

(2) Thoughts on Jesus Christ as our hope. His
name is "Emmanuel, which being interpreted is,
God with us" (Matt. 1:23). He is our teacher
(John 3:2). He was tempted in all points like as
we are (Heb. 4:15). He made choice of poverty
(II Cor. 8:9). He lived by the will of God (Matt.
26:39). He suffered for us (I Pet. 2:21). His
religion is a covenant of faith and pain. "For
unto you it is given in the behalf of Christ, not
only to believe on Him, but also to suffer for his
sake" (Phil. 1:29). If we are eager for money,
remember it was said of Him: He "hath not where
to lay his head" (Luke 9:58); if we are unfor-
giving, remember He prayed for his persecutors:
"Father, forgive them; for they know not what
they do" (Luke 23:34); if we long for a life of
ease and personal pleasure, remember that He says:

" No man, having put his hand to the plough, and looking back, is fit for the Kingdom of God " (Luke 9:62). However painful may be the contrast between Him and us, we must be courageous enough to face the differences, and ask ourselves if we are really willing to be more like Him. Because we have accepted a mild form of Christianity, it is no reason we should continue this mild form; we must follow Christ. " If any man will come after Me, let him deny himself, and take up his cross daily, and follow Me " (Luke 9:23).

(3) Thoughts on the Holy Spirit as our comforter. Jesus says: " He shall glorify Me; for He shall receive of mine, and shall show it unto thee " (John 16:14). Paul says: " If any man have not the Spirit of Christ, he is none of his " (Rom. 8:9). The universal hindrances to the reign of the Spirit in us are the lust of the flesh, the lust of the eyes, and the pride of life. These are our battle lines. " If ye through the Spirit do mortify the deeds of the body, ye shall live " (Rom. 8:13). " The world passeth away, and the lust thereof: but he that doeth the will of God abideth forever " (I John 2:17).

(4) Thoughts on the Church as composed of followers of Christ. " Christ loved the Church, and gave Himself for it " (Eph. 5:25). His love is upon all, however divided by theological controversies, national lines, and racial peculiarities. We must examine our hearts as to our attitude toward

other Christians, remembering that Christ says: "A
new commandment I give unto you, That ye love
one another; as I have loved you" (John 13:34).
Our lack of missionary enthusiasm and Christian
unity is due to our lack of spirituality. Therefore,
we must not be afraid to express repentance both
for our indifference in witnessing for Christ and
for our unbrotherly attitudes toward those who are
following Christ by other interpretations than our
own. If we have not learned to work with others,
we must examine our hearts to see if the fault does
not lie with us, rather than with others. Over us
still hovers the prayer of Jesus: "I pray . . .
that they all may be one; as Thou, Father, art in
Me, and I in Thee, that they also may be one in
Us: that the world may believe that Thou hast sent
Me" (John 17:21).

(5) Thoughts on the word of God as spiritual
nourishment. "Thy words were found, and I did
eat them" (Jer. 15:16). We only know the word
when we practice it. We must examine our hearts
to find why it is that we do not take the word of
God more seriously, why we content ourselves with
mild interpretations, and why we lack the courage
to apply it to our own lives. Wrote Edmond
Scherer, whose stumbling faith could not reach beyond human life: "If there is anything certain in
this world, it is that the destinies of the Bible are
linked with the destinies of holiness on earth." The
Psalmist says: "Thy word have I laid up in my

heart, that I might not sin against Thee" (Psa. 119:11).

(6) Thoughts on the reality of sin. "If we say that we have no sin, we deceive ourselves and the truth is not in us" (I John 1:8). The sins that are quite obvious are sexual vice, impurity, sensuality, jealousy, dissensions, quarrels, rivalry, temper, factions, envy, party spirit, covetousness, laziness, false-witness bearing, retaliation, revenge, revelry, and the like (Gal. 5:20, 21). These must be courageously faced by us, examining thoroughly their worth and consequences. Stock must be taken as to how large a place any of these has in our lives. The review must be tempered with charity, but we must command our will to such firmness that there will be a definite renunciation and abandonment. "If we confess our sins, He is faithful and just to forgive us our sins, and to cleanse us from all unrighteousness" (I John 1:9). The examination of conscience must be so thorough that conscience will be cleansed by Divine grace. God's forgiveness is always greater than our sins.

(7) Thoughts on the disaster of temptation. "Out of the heart proceed evil thoughts, murders, adulteries, fornications, thefts, false witness, blasphemies: these are the things which defile a man" (Matt. 15:19). Our common experience has taught us that the danger lies in taking pleasure in the thought of this, that, and the other sin, whether it be retaliation, revenge, sensuality, covetousness,

A RETREAT

jealousy, or what not. Our self-examination must
not be general; it must not be evasive; it must be
definite and tangible, inquiring as to how frequently we have invited temptation, or how frequently we have put up no protest when it ap-
proached, or how willingly we have yielded to its
demands. It is the struggle common to all mankind and differs only in that some are weaker at
one point than another. We must so examine ourselves that our weakest point may be made strong.
It demands courage. We must strike hard. Then,
set a watch, and pray that we may not go into the
struggle (Luke 22:40). Neither the severity of
the temptation nor its continuance should discourage us in continuing to try, nor estrange us from
our heavenly Father. " There hath no temptation
taken you but such as is common to man: but God
is faithful, who will not suffer you to be tempted
above that ye are able; but will with the temptation also make a way to escape, that ye may be
able to bear it " (I Cor. 10:13).

(8) Thoughts on the power of prayer. " Ask
and it shall be given you. . . . If ye then, being evil, know how to give good gifts unto your
children, how much more shall your Father who is
in heaven give good things to them that ask Him? "
(Matt. 7:7–11). However busy we may be, the
great principles of right living must not be ob-
scured by our activities, nor must they so distract
us that we do not find time to think of God and our

relations to Him. "Habits of dissipation and frivolity are peculiarly fatal to prayer. It should not need a violent wrench to recall us to the Divine Presence. The only way to pray well is to pray always. If our ordinary trend of thought is on a different plane from what is required in prayer, we cannot be surprised if we find prayer difficult. But the Christian who is inwardly and outwardly devout and recollected, comes to look on everything more and more in God, to pass easily from the creature to the Creator."[1] A retreat furnishes time for going over carefully the things of our ordinary occupations—not giving ourselves to daydreaming, but facing squarely, by prayer, the actual facts of the ordinary affairs of every-day life, and judging ourselves as we would judge another, were he doing what we are doing. The soul must make its approach to God in the attitude of genuine penitence and thanksgiving.

(9) Thoughts on the Lord's Supper as a covenant of grace. "To prepare for man upon this accursed earth a banquet of heavenly food—that cost Him much," says Andrew Murray. "Nothing less than the life and blood of his Son, to take away the curse and to open up to them the right and the access to heavenly blessings. Nothing less than the body and the blood of the Son of God could give life to lost men. O my soul, ponder the wonders

---

[1] Cuthbert Lattey, S. J. *Thy Love and Thy Grace* (Herder, London).

A RETREAT

of this royal banquet." [1]   As we look upon the symbols of this spiritual mystery, it is a call to the
crucifixion of self.   Paul says: " I am crucified
with Christ " (Gal. 2:20).   And of all Christians
he says: " They that are Christ's have crucified the
flesh with the affections and lusts " (Gal. 5:24).
Our difficulty is in remaining crucified; but here
again, a retreat challenges our right to lay down the
cross and to abandon the crucified life.   Out of the
atmosphere of Calvary grows the fruit of the Spirit,
which is love, joy, peace, good temper, kindliness,
generosity, fidelity, gentleness, and self-control
(Gal. 5:22, 23).   In the presence of this symbol
of his sufferings, we take stock of our spiritual
growth.   Christ must ever be the center of our
meditation.   In partaking of these symbols, we
have the consciousness both of the remission of our
sins and of the Living Presence (Matt. 26:28;
28:20).   Henceforth, we are hid with Christ in
God (Col. 3:3).   For us, He sanctified Himself
(John 17:17).   For his sake, we, in turn, must
prove our love for Him by the sanctifying of ourselves into the mystery of the Cross.   Only in this
atmosphere are we able to interpret at all the thir-
teenth chapter of first Corinthians, which may be
read and reread in our meditations at a retreat.

(10) Thoughts on spiritual resolution.   After a
full review of our meditation and self-examination
and prayer, and that without haste, we should de-

[1] Andrew Murray.   *The Lord's Table* (Nisbet, London).

[143]

liberately resolve to be more than we have been before. The resolution should be definite, perhaps
written out with no witness but God. It may hap-
pen that the resolution will be broken a short while
after it is made, leaving us discouraged and conscience stricken. We must, therefore, resolve again
—until seventy times seven is the way Christ talks
about it (Matt. 18:22). There is no limit. Browning well says:—

> When the fight begins within himself,
> A man's worth something.

That which is primary in us is not what we say or
do, but what we are—our character, and our out-
look upon life—all life—upon time and eternity.
Therefore, the call is to ourselves: " Choose you
this day whom ye will serve " (Josh. 24:15). The
fight is on. We must turn our backs to the foe
and remember that we are in Christ. Paul says:
" I cannot understand my own actions; I do not act
as I want to act; on the contrary, I do what I
detest. . . . In me (that is, in my flesh) no
good dwells, I know; the wish is there, but not the
power of doing what is right. I cannot be good
as I want to be, and I do wrong against my wishes.
Well, if I act against my wishes, it is not I who
do the deed but sin that dwells within me. So this
is my experience of the Law: I want to do what is
right, but wrong is all I can manage; I cordially
agree with God's law, so far as my inner self is

A RETREAT

concerned, but then I find quite another law in my
members which conflicts with the law of my mind
and makes me a prisoner to sin's law that resides
in my members. (Thus, left to myself, I serve the
law of God with my mind, but with my flesh I
serve the law of sin.) Miserable wretch that I am!
Who will rescue me from this body of death? God
will! Thanks be to Him through Jesus Christ our
Lord!"[1] (Rom. 7:15–25).

———

O God, whose way is altogether perfect, blot out
our transgressions according to the multitude of
thy tender mercies, and renew a right spirit within
us. Thou knowest that we want to do that which
is right, but we are frequently held in the thraldom
of sin. We understand neither thyself nor ourselves. Our ideals are holy, but we acknowledge
the lack of power to establish these ideals in our
lives. O Thou Redeeming God, rescue us from this
body of death, stand with us in the strife, endue us
with thy grace, and draw us to the mind of Jesus
Christ that He may be formed in us, and that Thou
mayest own us as thy children with Him, thy Son,
for surely thy goodness and lovingkindness shall
follow us all the days of our lives, and we shall
dwell in thy house for ever. Amen.

———
[1] Moffatt's Translation.

HOLY FATHER, we are conscious of sins that make us unworthy of thy love. We have followed too much the devices and desires of our own hearts. We have no worth that Thou shouldst accept us. Yet even in the midst of our ill desert, we are made aware by thy holy Word that if with all our hearts we truly seek Thee, we shall not seek in vain. Fulfil to us in this hour, we pray Thee, this gracious promise. We ask in Jesus' name. Amen.

—HERBERT L. WILLETT AND CHARLES CLAYTON MORRISON
(The Daily Altar—Christian Century Press).

XVIII

SELECTED PSALMS

PENITENTIAL PSALMS

" An Answer to Prayer " [1]

O Lord, rebuke me not in thine anger, neither chasten me in thy hot displeasure.

Have mercy upon me, O Lord; for I am weak: O Lord, heal me; for my bones are vexed.

My soul is also sore vexed: but Thou, O Lord, how long?

Return, O Lord, deliver my soul: oh save me for thy mercies' sake.

For in death there is no remembrance of Thee: in the grave who shall give Thee thanks?

I am weary with my groaning; all the night make I my bed to swim; I water my couch with my tears.

Mine eye is consumed because of grief; it waxeth old because of all mine enemies.

Depart from me, all ye workers of iniquity; for the Lord hath heard the voice of my weeping.

The Lord hath heard my supplication; the Lord will receive my prayer.

Let all mine enemies be ashamed and sore vexed: let them return and be ashamed suddenly.

—Psalm 6.

[1] Richard G. Moulton. *The Modern Reader's Bible* (Macmillan).

SELECTED PSALMS

"*Felicitations to the Forgiven*" [1]

Blessed is he whose transgression is forgiven, whose sin is covered.

Blessed is the man unto whom the Lord imputeth not iniquity, and in whose spirit there is no guile.

When I kept silence, my bones waxed old through my roaring all the day long.

For day and night thy hand was heavy upon me: my moisture is turned into the drought of summer.

I acknowledged my sin unto Thee, and mine iniquity have I not hid. I said, I will confess my transgressions unto the Lord; and Thou forgavest the iniquity of my sin.

For this shall every one that is godly pray unto Thee in a time when Thou mayest be found: surely in the floods of great waters they shall not come nigh unto him.

Thou art my hiding place; Thou shalt preserve me from trouble; Thou halt compass me about with songs of deliverance.

I will instruct thee and teach thee in the way which thou shalt go: I will guide thee with mine eye.

Be ye not as the horse, or as the mule, which have no understanding: whose mouth must be held in with bit and bridle, lest they come near unto thee.

Many sorrows shall be to the wicked: but he that trusteth in the Lord, mercy shall compass him about.

Be glad in the Lord, and rejoice, ye righteous: and shout for joy, all ye that are upright in heart.

—Psalm 32.

---

[1] J. B. Rotherham. *Studies in the Psalms* (Allenson).

PENITENTIAL PSALMS

An Elegy of a Troubled Heart

I said, I will take heed to my ways, that I sin not with my tongue: I will keep my mouth with a bridle, while the wicked is before me.

I was dumb with silence, I held my peace, even from good; and my sorrow was stirred.

My heart was hot within me; while I was musing the fire burned: then spake I with my tongue,

Lord, make me to know mine end, and the measure of my days, what it is; that I may know how frail I am.

Behold, Thou hast made my days as a handbreadth; and mine age is as nothing before Thee: verily every man at his best state is altogether vanity.

Surely every man walketh in a vain shew: surely they are disquieted in vain: he heapeth up riches, and knoweth not who shall gather them.

And now, Lord, what wait I for? my hope is in Thee.

Deliver me from all my transgressions: make me not the reproach of the foolish.

I was dumb, I opened not my mouth; because Thou didst it.

Remove thy stroke away from me: I am con-- sumed by the blow of thine hand.

When Thou with rebukes dost correct man for iniquity, thou makest his beauty to consume away like a moth: surely every man is vanity. Selah.

Hear my prayer, O Lord, and give ear unto my cry; hold not thy peace at my tears: for I am a stranger with Thee, and a sojourner, as all my fathers were.

O spare me, that I may recover strength, before I go hence, and be no more.

—Psalm 39.

———

"Corruption Within and Foes Without" [1]

O Lord, rebuke me not in thy wrath: neither chasten me in thy hot displeasure.

For thine arrows stick fast in me, and thy hand presseth me sore.

There is no soundness in my flesh because of thine anger; neither is there any rest in my bones because of my sin.

For mine iniquities are gone over mine head: as a heavy burden they are too heavy for me.

My wounds stink and are corrupt because of my foolishness.

I am troubled; I am bowed down greatly; I go mourning all the day long.

For my loins are filled with a loathsome disease: and there is no soundness in my flesh.

I am feeble and sore broken: I have roared by reason of the disquietness of my heart.

Lord, all my desire is before Thee; and my groaning is not hid from Thee.

---

[1] Richard G. Moulton. *The Modern Reader's Bible* (Macmillan).

PENITENTIAL PSALMS

My heart panteth, my strength faileth me: as for the light of mine eyes, it also is gone from me.

My lovers and my friends stand aloof from my sore; and my kinsmen stand afar off.

They also that seek after my life lay snares for me; and they that seek my hurt speak mischievous things, and imagine deceits all the day long.

But I, as a deaf man, heard not; and I was as a dumb man that openeth not his mouth.

Thus I was as a man that heareth not, and in whose mouth are no reproofs.

For in Thee, O Lord, do I hope: Thou wilt hear, O Lord my God.

For I said, Hear me, lest otherwise they should rejoice over me: when my foot slippeth, they magnify themselves against me.

For I am ready to halt, and my sorrow is continually before me.

For I will declare mine iniquity; I will be sorry for my sin.

But mine enemies are lively, and they are strong: and they that hate me wrongfully are multiplied.

They also that render evil for good are mine adversaries; because I follow the thing that good is.

Forsake me not, O Lord: O my God, be not far from me.

Make haste to help me, O Lord my salvation.

—Psalm 38.

The Prodigal's Psalm

Have mercy upon me, O God, according to thy lovingkindness: according unto the multitude of thy tender mercies blot out my transgressions.

Wash me thoroughly from mine iniquity, and cleanse me from my sin.

For I acknowledge my transgressions and my sin is ever before me.

Against Thee, Thee only, have I sinned, and done this evil in thy sight: that Thou mightest be justified when Thou speakest, and be clear when Thou judgest.

Behold, I was shapen in iniquity; and in sin did my mother conceive me.

Behold, Thou desirest truth in the inward parts: and in the hidden part Thou shalt make me to know wisdom.

Purge me with hyssop, and I shall be clean: wash me, and I shall be whiter than snow.

Make me to hear joy and gladness; that the bones which Thou hast broken may rejoice.

Hide thy face from my sins, and blot out all mine iniquities.

Create in me a clean heart, O God; and renew a right spirit within me.

Cast me not away from thy presence; and take not thy Holy Spirit from me.

Restore unto me the joy of thy salvation; and uphold me with thy free Spirit.

Then will I teach transgressors thy ways, and sinners shall be converted unto Thee.

Deliver me from bloodguiltiness, O God, Thou God of my salvation: and my tongue shall sing aloud of thy righteousness.

O Lord, open Thou my lips; and my mouth shall shew forth thy praise.

For Thou desirest not sacrifice; else would I give it: Thou delightest not in burnt offering.

The sacrifices of God are a broken spirit: a broken and a contrite heart, O God, Thou wilt not despise.

Do good in thy good pleasure unto Zion: build Thou the walls of Jerusalem.

Then shalt Thou be pleased with the sacrifices of righteousness, with burnt offering and whole burnt offering: then shall they offer bullocks upon thine altar.

—Psalm 51.

The Sighing of the Disconsolate

Hear my prayer, O Lord, and let my cry come unto Thee.

Hide not thy face from me in the day when I am in trouble; incline thine ear unto me: in the day when I call answer me speedily.

For my days are consumed like smoke, and my bones are burned as an hearth.

My heart is smitten, and withered like grass; so that I forget to eat my bread.

By reason of the voice of my groaning my bones cleave to my skin.

I am like a pelican of the wilderness: I am like an owl of the desert.

I watch, and am as a sparrow alone upon the housetop.

Mine enemies reproach me all the day; and they that are mad against me are sworn against me.

For I have eaten ashes like bread, and mingled my drink with weeping,

Because of thine indignation and thy wrath: for Thou hast lifted me up, and cast me down.

My days are like a shadow that declineth; and I am withered like grass.

But Thou, O Lord, shalt endure for ever; and thy remembrance unto all generations.

Thou shalt arise, and have mercy upon Zion: for the time to favour her, yea, the set time, is come.

For thy servants take pleasure in her stones, and favour the dust thereof.

So the heathen shall fear the name of the Lord, and all the kings of the earth thy glory.

When the Lord shall build up Zion, He shall appear in his glory.

He will regard the prayer of the destitute, and not despise their prayer.

This shall be written for the generation to come: and the people which shall be created shall praise the Lord.

For He hath looked down from the height of his

sanctuary; from heaven did the Lord behold the earth;

To hear the groaning of the prisoner; to loose those that are appointed to death;

To declare the name of the Lord in Zion, and his praise in Jerusalem;

When the people are gathered together, and the kingdoms, to serve the Lord.

He weakened my strength in the way; He short-ened my days.

I said, O my God, take me not away in the midst of my days: thy years are throughout all genera-tions.

Of old hast Thou laid the foundation of the earth: and the heavens are the work of thy hands.

They shall perish, but Thou shalt endure: yea, all of them shall wax old like a garment; as a vesture shalt Thou change them, and they shall be changed:

But Thou art the same, and thy years shall have no end.

The children of thy servants shall continue, and their seed shall be established before Thee.

—Psalm 102.

_____

" A Pauline Psalm on Forgiveness " [1]

Out of the depths have I cried unto Thee, O Lord.

Lord, hear my voice: let thine ears be attentive to the voice of my supplications.

_____
[1] Martin Luther.

If Thou, Lord, shouldest mark iniquities, O Lord, who shall stand?

But there is forgiveness with Thee, that Thou mayest be feared.

I wait for the Lord, my soul doth wait, and in his word do I hope.

My soul waiteth for the Lord more than they that watch for the morning: I say, more than they that watch for the morning.

Let Israel hope in the Lord: for with the Lord there is mercy, and with Him is plenteous redemption.

And He shall redeem Israel from all his iniquities.
—*Psalm 130.*

———

The Lifting Up of the Soul in Distress

Hear my prayer, O Lord, give ear to my supplications: in thy faithfulness answer me, and in thy righteousness.

And enter not into judgment with thy servant: for in thy sight shall no man living be justified.

For the enemy hath persecuted my soul; he hath smitten my life down to the ground; he hath made me to dwell in darkness, as those that have been long dead.

Therefore is my spirit overwhelmed within me; my heart within me is desolate.

I remember the days of old; I meditate on all thy works; I muse on the work of thy hands.

[156]

PENITENTIAL PSALMS

I stretch forth my hands unto Thee: my soul thirsteth after Thee, as a thirsty land.

Hear me speedily, O Lord; my spirit faileth: hide not thy face from me, lest I be like unto them that go down into the pit.

Cause me to hear thy lovingkindness in the morning; for in Thee do I trust: cause me to know the way wherein I should walk; for I lift up my soul unto Thee.

Deliver me, O Lord, from mine enemies: I flee unto Thee to hide me.

Teach me to do thy will; for Thou art my God: thy Spirit is good; lead me into the land of uprightness.

Quicken me, O Lord, for thy name's sake: for thy righteousness' sake bring my soul out of trouble.

—Psalm 143.

My Father, I thank Thee for all the mercies of the past. Quicken my memory that I may recall them. May I see the way of grace along which Thou hast in mercy led me! May thy mercy awake my praise! I turn to the day's work, I turn to the earning of my daily bread. May I go to it as to prayer! May my labour be an act of worship! May the spirit of my toil rise as acceptable fragrance to Thee! Father of lights, I thank Thee for every one who brings me any illumination. For all who bring me suggestion, counsel, warning; for all who help me by voice or by pen; for all who lead me into a larger life, I give Thee the praise and glory. Amen.

—J. H. Jowett *(Yet Another Day—Revell).*

THANKSGIVING PSALMS

An Anthem of Remembrance

I will extol Thee, O Lord; for Thou hast lifted me up, and hast not made my foes to rejoice over me.

O Lord my God, I cried unto Thee, and Thou hast healed me.

O Lord, Thou hast brought up my soul from the grave: Thou hast kept me alive, that I should not go down to the pit.

Sing unto the Lord, O ye saints of his, and give thanks at the remembrance of his holiness.

For his anger endureth but a moment; in his favour is life: weeping may endure for a night, but joy cometh in the morning.

And in my prosperity I said, I shall never be moved.

Lord, by thy favour Thou hast made my mountain to stand strong: Thou didst hide thy face, and I was troubled.

I cried to Thee, O Lord; and unto the Lord I made supplication.

What profit is there in my blood, when I go down to the pit? Shall the dust praise Thee? shall it declare thy truth?

Hear, O Lord, and have mercy upon me: Lord, be Thou my helper.

Thou hast turned for me my mourning into dancing: Thou hast put off my sackcloth, and girded me with gladness;

To the end that my glory may sing praise to Thee, and not be silent. O Lord my God, I will give thanks unto Thee for ever.

—Psalm 30.

" The City of Immanuel " [1]

God is our refuge and strength, a very present help in trouble.

Therefore will not we fear, though the earth be removed, and though the mountains be carried into the midst of the sea;

Though the waters thereof roar and be troubled, though the mountains shake with the swelling thereof.

There is a river, the streams whereof shall make glad the city of God, the holy place of the tabernacles of the Most High.

God is in the midst of her; she shall not be moved: God shall help her, and that right early.

The heathen raged, the kingdoms were moved: He uttered his voice, the earth melted.

The Lord of hosts is with us; the God of Jacob is our refuge.

Come, behold the works of the Lord, what desolations He hath made in the earth.

He maketh wars to cease unto the end of the

[1] Henry van Dyke. *The Story of the Psalms* (Scribner).

earth; He breaketh the bow, and cutteth the spear in sunder; He burneth the chariot in the fire.

Be still, and know that I am God: I will be exalted among the heathen, I will be exalted in the earth.

The Lord of hosts is with us; the God of Jacob is our refuge.

—Psalm 46.

"Grateful Acknowledgment of Seedtime and Harvest" [1]

Praise waiteth for Thee, O God, in Zion: and unto Thee shall the vow be performed.

O Thou that hearest prayer, unto Thee shall all flesh come.

Iniquities prevail against me: as for our transgressions, Thou shalt purge them away.

Blessed is the man whom Thou choosest, and causest to approach unto Thee, that he may dwell in thy courts: we shall be satisfied with the goodness of thy house, even of thy holy temple.

By terrible things in righteousness wilt Thou answer us, O God of our salvation; who art the confidence of all the ends of the earth, and of them that are afar off upon the sea:

Which by his strength setteth fast the mountains; being girded with power:

Which stilleth the noise of the seas, the noise of their waves, and the tumult of the people.

---

[1] J. B. Rotherham. *Studies in the Psalms* (Allenson).

They also that dwell in the uttermost parts are afraid at thy tokens: Thou makest the outgoings of the morning and evening to rejoice.

Thou visitest the earth, and waterest it: Thou greatly enrichest it with the river of God, which is full of water: Thou preparest them corn, when Thou hast so provided for it.

Thou waterest the ridges thereof abundantly: Thou settlest the furrows thereof: Thou makest it soft with showers: Thou blessest the springing thereof.

Thou crownest the year with thy goodness; and thy paths drop fatness.

They drop upon the pastures of the wilderness: and the little hills rejoice on every side.

The pastures are clothed with flocks; the valleys also are covered over with corn; they shout for joy, they also sing.

—Psalm 65.

———

A Votive Hymn of Invitation to All to Join in Praise to God

Make a joyful noise unto God, all ye lands:

Sing forth the honour of his name: make his praise glorious.

Say unto God, How terrible art Thou in thy works! through the greatness of thy power shall thine enemies submit themselves unto Thee.

All the earth shall worship Thee, and shall sing unto Thee; they shall sing to thy name.

THANKSGIVING PSALMS

Come and see the works of God: He is terrible in his doing toward the children of men.

He turned the sea into dry land: they went through the flood on foot: there did we rejoice in Him.

He ruleth by his power for ever; his eyes behold the nations: let not the rebellious exalt themselves.

O bless our God, ye people, and make the voice of his praise to be heard:

Which holdeth our soul in life, and suffereth not our feet to be moved.

For Thou, O God, hast proved us: Thou hast tried us, as silver is tried.

Thou broughtest us into the net; Thou laidst affliction upon our loins.

Thou hast caused men to ride over our heads; we went through fire and through water: but Thou broughtest us out into a wealthy place.

I will go into thy house with burnt offerings: I will pay Thee my vows,

Which my lips have uttered, and my mouth hath spoken, when I was in trouble.

Come and hear, all ye that fear God, and I will declare what He hath done for my soul.

I cried unto Him with my mouth, and He was extolled with my tongue.

If I regard iniquity in my heart, the Lord will not hear me:

But verily God hath heard me; He hath attended to the voice of my prayer.

Blessed be God, which hath not turned away my prayer, nor his mercy from me.

—Psalm 66.

A Festal Response on Longing to See God Worshipped by All

God be merciful unto us, and bless us; and cause his face to shine upon us;

That thy way may be known upon earth, thy saving health among all nations.

Let the people praise Thee, O God; let all the people praise Thee.

O let the nations be glad and sing for joy: for Thou shalt judge the people righteously, and govern the nations upon earth.

Let the people praise Thee, O God; let all the people praise Thee.

Then shall the earth yield her increase; and God, even our own God, shall bless us.

God shall bless us; and all the ends of the earth shall fear Him.

—Psalm 67.

Joyful Tidings of the Coming Kingdom

O sing unto the Lord a new song: sing unto the Lord, all the earth.

Sing unto the Lord, bless his name; show forth his salvation from day to day.

Declare his glory among the heathen, his wonders among all people.

THANKSGIVING PSALMS

For the Lord is great, and greatly to be praised:
He is to be feared above all gods.

For all the gods of the nations are idols: but the
Lord made the heavens.

Honour and majesty are before Him: strength
and beauty are in his sanctuary.

Give unto the Lord, O ye kindreds of the people,
give unto the Lord glory and strength.

Give unto the Lord the glory due unto his name:
bring an offering, and come into his courts.

O worship the Lord in the beauty of holiness: fear
before Him, all the earth.

Say among the heathen that the Lord reigneth:
the world also shall be established that it shall not
be moved: He shall judge the people righteously.

Let the heavens rejoice, and let the earth be
glad; let the sea roar, and the fulness thereof.

Let the field be joyful, and all that is therein:
then shall all the trees of the wood rejoice

Before the Lord: for He cometh, for He cometh
to judge the earth: He shall judge the world with
righteousness, and the people with his truth.

—Psalm 96.

" The Praise of Prayer " [1]

O give thanks unto the Lord, for He is good: for
his mercy endureth for ever.

Let the redeemed of the Lord say so, whom He
hath redeemed from the hand of the enemy;

[1] Henry van Dyke. *The Story of the Psalms* (Scribner).

And gathered them out of the lands, from the east, and from the west, from the north, and from the south.

They wandered in the wilderness in a solitary way; they found no city to dwell in.

Hungry and thirsty, their soul fainted in them.

Then they cried unto the Lord in their trouble, and He delivered them out of their distresses.

And He led them forth by the right way, that they might go to a city of habitation.

Oh that men would praise the Lord for his goodness, and for his wonderful works to the children of men!

For He satisfieth the longing soul, and filleth the hungry soul with goodness.

Such as sit in darkness and in the shadow of death, being bound in affliction and iron;

Because they rebelled against the words of God, and contemned the counsel of the Most High:

Therefore He brought down their heart with labour; they fell down, and there was none to help.

Then they cried unto the Lord in their trouble, and He saved them out of their distresses.

He brought them out of darkness and the shadow of death, and brake their bands in sunder.

Oh that men would praise the Lord for his goodness, and for his wonderful works to the children of men!

For He hath broken the gates of brass, and cut the bars of iron in sunder.

THANKSGIVING PSALMS

Fools, because of their transgression, and because of their iniquities, are afflicted.

Their soul abhorreth all manner of meat; and they draw near unto the gates of death.

Then they cry unto the Lord in their trouble, and He saveth them out of their distresses.

He sent His word, and healed them, and delivered them from their destructions.

Oh that men would praise the Lord for his goodness, and for his wonderful works to the children of men!

And let them sacrifice the sacrifices of thanksgiving, and declare his works with rejoicing.

They that go down to the sea in ships, that do business in great waters;

These see the works of the Lord, and his wonders in the deep.

For He commandeth, and raiseth the stormy wind, which lifteth up the waves thereof.

They mount up to the heaven, they go down again to the depths: their soul is melted because of trouble.

They reel to and fro, and stagger like a drunken man, and are at their wit's end.

Then they cry unto the Lord in their trouble, and He bringeth them out of their distresses.

He maketh the storm a calm, so that the waves thereof are still.

Then are they glad because they be quiet; so He bringeth them unto their desired haven.

SELECTED PSALMS

Oh that men would praise the Lord for his goodness, and for his wonderful works to the children of men!

Let them exalt Him also in the congregation of the people, and praise Him in the assembly of the elders.

He turneth rivers into a wilderness, and the watersprings into dry ground;

A fruitful land into barrenness, for the wickedness of them that dwell therein.

He turneth the wilderness into a standing water, and dry ground into watersprings.

And there He maketh the hungry to dwell, that they may prepare a city for habitation;

And sow the fields, and plant vineyards, which may yield fruits of increase.

He blesseth them also, so that they are multiplied greatly; and suffereth not their cattle to decrease.

Again, they are minished and brought low through oppression, affliction, and sorrow.

He poureth contempt upon princes, and causeth them to wander in the wilderness, where there is no way.

Yet setteth He the poor on high from affliction, and maketh him families like a flock.

The righteous shall see it, and rejoice: and all iniquity shall stop her mouth.

Whoso is wise, and will observe these things, even they shall understand the lovingkindness of the Lord.

—Psalm 107.

THANKSGIVING PSALMS

A Votive Hymn for Deliverance from Death

I love the Lord, because He hath heard my voice and my supplications.

Because He hath inclined his ear unto me, therefore will I call upon Him as long as I live.

The sorrows of death compassed me, and the pains of hell gat hold upon me: I found trouble and sorrow.

Then called I upon the name of the Lord; O Lord, I beseech Thee, deliver my soul.

Gracious is the Lord, and righteous; yea, our God is merciful.

The Lord preserveth the simple: I was brought low, and He helped me.

Return unto thy rest, O my soul; for the Lord hath dealt bountifully with thee.

For Thou hast delivered my soul from death, mine eyes from tears, and my feet from falling.

I will walk before the Lord in the land of the living.

I believed, therefore have I spoken: I was greatly afflicted:

I said in my haste, All men are liars.

What shall I render unto the Lord for all his benefits toward me?

I will take the cup of salvation, and call upon the name of the Lord.

I will pay my vows unto the Lord now in the presence of all his people.

—*Psalm 116.*

SELECTED PSALMS

Thanksgiving for Sudden Deliverance

If it had not been the Lord who was on our side, now may Israel say;

If it had not been the Lord who was on our side, when men rose up against us:

Then they had swallowed us up quick, when their wrath was kindled against us:

Then the waters had overwhelmed us, the stream had gone over our soul:

Then the proud waters had gone over our soul.

Blessed be the Lord, who hath not given us as a prey to their teeth.

Our soul is escaped as a bird out of the snare of the fowlers: the snare is broken, and we are escaped.

Our help is in the name of the Lord, who made heaven and earth.

—Psalm 124.

————

The Certainty of God's Response

I will praise Thee with my whole heart: before the gods will I sing praise unto Thee.

I will worship toward thy holy temple, and praise thy name for thy lovingkindness and for thy truth: for Thou hast magnified thy word above all thy name.

In the day when I cried Thou answeredst me, and strengthenedst me with strength in my soul.

THANKSGIVING PSALMS

All the kings of the earth shall praise Thee, O Lord, when they hear the words of thy mouth.

Yea, they shall sing in the ways of the Lord: for great is the glory of the Lord.

Though the Lord be high, yet hath He respect unto the lowly: but the proud He knoweth afar off.

Though I walk in the midst of trouble, Thou wilt revive me: Thou shalt stretch forth thine hand against the wrath of mine enemies, and thy right hand shall save me.

The Lord will perfect that which concerneth me: thy mercy, O Lord, endureth for ever: forsake not the works of thine own hands.

—Psalm 138.

O LORD, Thou art our refuge in every time of trouble and of danger. Though we forget Thee, too often, when our path is unshadowed, and all goes well with us, yet in the day of affliction, when clouds overspread our sky, Thou art remembered by us as our only refuge, and to Thee we flee. Gracious Father, hear us, when we call upon Thee, and grant us thy protection. Help me, dear Father, in the midst of distress and danger and care, to trust Thee more fully, and to commit myself to thy care in filial confidence. May I be able to realize more fully than I have ever done that " all things work together for good to them that love God and are the called according to his purpose." Help me to feel that underneath me at all times are the everlasting arms. So shall I have peace and rest. Keep me, O Lord, under the shadow of thy wings, until life's storms be overpast, and bring me with all thy faithful ones, to the peaceful haven of everlasting rest; through Jesus Christ, to whom be glory, for ever and ever. Amen.

—J. H. GARRISON *(Alone With God—*
Christian Board of Publication).

PETITION PSALMS

The Lifting Up of the Soul in Supplication

Unto Thee, O Lord, do I lift up my soul.

O my God, I trust in Thee: let me not be ashamed, let not mine enemies triumph over me.

Yea, let none that wait on Thee be ashamed: let them be ashamed which transgress without cause.

Shew me thy ways, O Lord; teach me thy paths.

Lead me in thy truth, and teach me: for Thou art the God of my salvation; on Thee do I wait all the day.

Remember, O Lord, thy tender mercies and thy lovingkindnesses; for they have been ever of old.

Remember not the sins of my youth, nor my transgressions: according to thy mercy remember Thou me for thy goodness' sake, O Lord.

Good and upright is the Lord: therefore will He teach sinners in the way.

The meek will He guide in judgment: and the meek will He teach his way.

All the paths of the Lord are mercy and truth unto such as keep his covenant and his testimonies.

For thy name's sake, O Lord, pardon mine iniquity; for it is great.

What man is he that feareth the Lord? him shall He teach in the way that He shall choose.

His soul shall dwell at ease; and his seed shall inherit the earth.

The secret of the Lord is with them that fear Him; and He will shew them his covenant.

Mine eyes are ever toward the Lord; for He shall pluck my feet out of the net.

Turn Thee unto me, and have mercy upon me; for I am desolate and afflicted.

The troubles of my heart are enlarged: O bring Thou me out of my distresses.

Look upon mine affliction and my pain; and forgive all my sins.

Consider mine enemies; for they are many; and they hate me with cruel hatred.

O keep my soul, and deliver me: let me not be ashamed; for I put my trust in Thee.

Let integrity and uprightness preserve me; for I wait on Thee.

Redeem Israel, O God, out of all his troubles.

—Psalm 25.

———

"*A Sufferer's Consolation*" [1]

Blessed is he that considereth the poor: the Lord will deliver him in time of trouble.

The Lord will preserve him, and keep him alive; and he shall be blessed upon the earth: and Thou wilt not deliver him unto the will of his enemies.

The Lord will strengthen him upon the bed of

---

[1] *The New-Century Bible* (Froude).

languishing: Thou wilt make all his bed in his sickness.

I said, Lord, be merciful unto me: heal my soul; for I have sinned against Thee.

Mine enemies speak evil of me, When shall he die, and his name perish?

And if he come to see me, he speaketh vanity: his heart gathereth iniquity to itself; when he goeth abroad, he telleth it.

All that hate me whisper together against me: against me do they devise my hurt.

An evil disease, say they, cleaveth fast unto him: and now that he lieth he shall rise up no more.

Yea, mine own familiar friend, in whom I trusted, which did eat of my bread, hath lifted up his heel against me.

But Thou, O Lord, be merciful unto me, and raise me up, that I may requite them.

By this I know that Thou favourest me, because mine enemy doth not triumph over me.

And as for me, Thou upholdest me in mine integrity, and settest me before thy face for ever.

Blessed be the Lord God of Israel from everlasting, and to everlasting. Amen, and Amen.

—Psalm 41.

The Leading of Light and Truth

Judge me, O God, and plead my cause against an ungodly nation: O deliver me from the deceitful and unjust man.

For Thou art the God of my strength: why dost Thou cast me off? why go I mourning because of the oppression of the enemy?

O send out thy light and thy truth: let them lead me; let them bring me unto thy holy hill, and to thy tabernacles.

Then will I go unto the altar of God, unto God my exceeding joy: yea, upon the harp will I praise Thee, O God my God.

Why art thou cast down, O my soul? and why art thou disquieted within me? hope in God: for I shall yet praise Him, who is the health of my countenance, and my God.

—*Psalm 43.*

"*A Prayer Without a Petition*"[1]

O God, Thou art my God; early will I seek Thee: my soul thirsteth for Thee, my flesh longeth for Thee in a dry and thirsty land, where no water is;

To see thy power and thy glory, so as I have seen Thee in the sanctuary.

Because thy lovingkindness is better than life, my lips shall praise Thee.

Thus will I bless Thee while I live: I will lift up my hands in thy name.

My soul shall be satisfied as with marrow and fatness; and my mouth shall praise Thee with joyful lips:

[1] Henry van Dyke. *The Story of the Psalms* (Scribner).

When I remember Thee upon my bed, and meditate on Thee in the night watches.

Because Thou hast been my help, therefore in the shadow of thy wings will I rejoice.

My soul followeth hard after Thee: thy right hand upholdeth me.

But those that seek my soul, to destroy it, shall go into the lower parts of the earth.

They shall fall by the sword: they shall be a portion for foxes.

But the king shall rejoice in God; every one that sweareth by Him shall glory: but the mouth of them that speak lies shall be stopped.

—*Psalm 63.*

A Faithful Servant Casting Himself on the Mercy of God

Bow down thine ear, O Lord, hear me: for I am poor and needy.

Preserve my soul; for I am holy: O Thou my God, save thy servant that trusteth in Thee.

Be merciful unto me, O Lord: for I cry unto Thee daily.

Rejoice the soul of thy servant: for unto Thee, O Lord, do I lift up my soul.

For Thou, Lord, art good, and ready to forgive; and plenteous in mercy unto all them that call upon Thee.

Give ear, O Lord, unto my prayer; and attend to the voice of my supplications.

SELECTED PSALMS

In the day of my trouble I will call upon Thee: for Thou wilt answer me.

Among the gods there is none like unto Thee, O Lord; neither are there any works like unto thy works.

All nations whom Thou hast made shall come and worship before Thee, O Lord; and shall glorify thy name.

For Thou art great, and doest wondrous things: Thou art God alone.

Teach me thy way, O Lord; I will walk in thy truth: unite my heart to fear thy name.

I will praise Thee, O Lord my God, with all my heart: and I will glorify thy name for evermore.

For great is thy mercy toward me: and Thou hast delivered my soul from the lowest hell.

O God, the proud are risen against me, and the assemblies of violent men have sought after my soul; and have not set Thee before them.

But Thou, O Lord, art a God full of compassion, and gracious, longsuffering, and plenteous in mercy and truth.

O turn unto me, and have mercy upon me; give thy strength unto thy servant, and save the son of thine handmaid.

Shew me a token for good; that they which hate me may see it, and be ashamed: because Thou, Lord, hast holpen me, and comforted me.

—*Psalm 86.*

PETITION PSALMS

A Petition for Understanding

Teach me, O Lord, the way of thy statutes; and I shall keep it unto the end.

Give me understanding, and I shall keep thy law; yea, I shall observe it with my whole heart.

Make me to go in the path of thy commandments; for therein do I delight.

Incline my heart unto thy testimonies, and not to covetousness.

Turn away mine eyes from beholding vanity; and quicken Thou me in thy way.

Stablish thy word unto thy servant, who is devoted to thy fear.

Turn away my reproach which I fear: for thy judgments are good.

Behold, I have longed after thy precepts: quicken me in thy righteousness.

—Psalm 119: 33–40.

" A Prayer of the Despised " [1]

Unto Thee lift I up mine eyes, O Thou that dwellest in the heavens.

Behold, as the eyes of servants look unto the hand of their masters, and as the eyes of a maiden unto the hand of her mistress; so our eyes wait upon the Lord our God, until that He have mercy upon us.

[1] Richard G. Moulton. *The Modern Reader's Bible* (Macmillan).

Have mercy upon us, O Lord, have mercy upon us: for we are exceedingly filled with contempt.

Our soul is exceedingly filled with the scorning of those that are at ease, and with the contempt of the proud. —*Psalm 123*.

———

Prayerful Caution in the Use of the Tongue

Lord, I cry unto Thee: make haste unto me; give ear unto my voice, when I cry unto Thee.

Let my prayer be set forth before Thee as incense; and the lifting up of my hands as the evening sacrifice.

Set a watch, O Lord, before my mouth; keep the door of my lips.

Incline not my heart to any evil thing, to practise wicked works with men that work iniquity: and let me not eat of their dainties.

Let the righteous smite me; it shall be a kindness: and let him reprove me; it shall be an excellent oil, which shall not break my head: for yet my prayer also shall be in their calamities.

When their judges are overthrown in stony places, they shall hear my words; for they are sweet.

Our bones are scattered at the grave's mouth, as when one cutteth and cleaveth wood upon the earth.

But mine eyes are unto Thee, O God the Lord: in Thee is my trust; leave not my soul destitute.

Keep me from the snares which they have laid for me, and the gins of the workers of iniquity.

PETITION PSALMS

Let the wicked fall into their own nets, whilst that I withal escape.

—*Psalm 141.*

————

A Voice of Loneliness

I cried unto the Lord with my voice; with my voice unto the Lord did I make my supplication.

I poured out my complaint before Him; I shewed before Him my trouble.

When my spirit was overwhelmed within me, then Thou knewest my path. In the way wherein I walked have they privily laid a snare for me.

I looked on my right hand, and beheld, but there was no man that would know me: refuge failed me; no man cared for my soul.

I cried unto Thee, O Lord: I said, Thou art my refuge and my portion in the land of the living.

Attend unto my cry; for I am brought very low: deliver me from my persecutors; for they are stronger than I.

Bring my soul out of prison, that I may praise thy name: the righteous shall compass me about; for Thou shalt deal bountifully with me.

—*Psalm 142.*

O LORD, we thank Thee for the beginnings as well as for the end of things, for processes as well as for results, for seedtime as well as for harvest, and especially for the days of growth. Let the beauty of the summertide and the broadening of the leaves speak to our hearts of thy unceasing care. Forgive us our forgetful hours and by thy mercy turn complaints to praise. How wonderful are all thy works that we behold! Teach us to expect new wonders as we see more of Thee. And may we by thy good Spirit grow in wisdom as we grow in years, becoming childlike in our faith and expectation, as becometh thy children and the followers of our Elder Brother, Christ. In his name. Amen.

—ISAAC OGDEN RANKIN *(A Diary for the Thankful Hearted by Mary Hodgkin—Methuen).*

NATURE PSALMS

God in Nature

O Lord our Lord, how excellent is thy name in all the earth! who hast set thy glory above the heavens.

Out of the mouth of babes and sucklings hast Thou ordained strength because of thine enemies, that Thou mightest still the enemy and the avenger.

When I consider thy heavens, the work of thy fingers, the moon and the stars, which Thou hast ordained;

What is man, that Thou art mindful of him? and the son of man, that Thou visitest him?

For thou hast made him a little lower than the angels, and hast crowned him with glory and honour.

Thou madest him to have dominion over the works of thy hands; Thou hast put all things under his feet:

All sheep and oxen, yea, and the beasts of the field;

The fowl of the air, and the fish of the sea, and whatsoever passeth through the paths of the seas.

O Lord our Lord, how excellent is thy name in all the earth!

—Psalm 8.

SELECTED PSALMS

" The Heavens Above and the Law Within " [1]

The heavens declare the glory of God; and the firmament sheweth his handywork.

Day unto day uttereth speech, and night unto night sheweth knowledge.

There is no speech nor language, where their voice is not heard.

Their line is gone out through all the earth, and their words to the end of the world. In them hath He set a tabernacle for the sun,

Which is as a bridegroom coming out of his chamber, and rejoiceth as a strong man to run a race.

His going forth is from the end of the heaven, and his circuit unto the ends if it: and there is nothing hid from the heat thereof.

The law of the Lord is perfect, converting the soul: the testimony of the Lord is sure, making wise the simple.

The statutes of the Lord are right, rejoicing the heart: the commandment of the Lord is pure, enlightening the eyes.

The fear of the Lord is clean, enduring for ever: the judgments of the Lord are true and righteous altogether.

More to be desired are they than gold, yea, than much fine gold: sweeter also than honey and the honeycomb.

---

[1] Richard G. Moulton. *The Modern Reader's Bible* (Macmillan).

Moreover by them is thy servant warned: and in keeping of them there is great reward.

Who can understand his errors? cleanse Thou me from secret faults.

Keep back thy servant also from presumptuous sins; let them not have dominion over me: then shall I be upright, and I shall be innocent from the great transgression.

Let the words of my mouth, and the meditation of my heart, be acceptable in thy sight, O Lord, my strength, and my redeemer.

—Psalm 19.

God in the Storm

Give unto the Lord, O ye mighty, give unto the Lord glory and strength.

Give unto the Lord the glory due unto his name; worship the Lord in the beauty of holiness.

The voice of the Lord is upon the waters: the God of glory thundereth: the Lord is upon many waters.

The voice of the Lord is powerful; the voice of the Lord is full of majesty.

The voice of the Lord breaketh the cedars; yea, the Lord breaketh the cedars of Lebanon.

He maketh them also to skip like a calf; Lebanon and Sirion like a young unicorn.

The voice of the Lord divideth the flames of fire.

The voice of the Lord shaketh the wilderness; the Lord shaketh the wilderness of Kadesh.

The voice of the Lord maketh the hinds to calve, and discovereth the forests: and in his temple doth every one speak of his glory.

The Lord sitteth upon the flood; yea, the Lord sitteth King for ever.

The Lord will give strength unto his people; the Lord will bless his people with peace. —*Psalm 29.*

The Voice of the Waters

The Lord reigneth, He is clothed with majesty; the Lord is clothed with strength, wherewith He hath girded Himself: the world also is stablished, that it cannot be moved.

Thy throne is established of old: Thou art from everlasting.

The floods have lifted up, O Lord, the floods have lifted up their voice; the floods lift up their waves.

The Lord on high is mightier than the noise of many waters, yea, than the mighty waves of the sea.

Thy testimonies are very sure: holiness becometh thine house, O Lord, for ever.

—*Psalm 93.*

" An Ode of Creation "[1]

Bless the Lord, O my soul. O Lord my God, Thou art very great; Thou art clothed with honour and majesty:

Who coverest thyself with light as with a gar-

[1] J. J. S. Perowne. *The Book of Psalms* (Draper).

ment: who stretchest out the heavens like a curtain:

Who layeth the beams of his chambers in the waters: who maketh the clouds his chariot: who walketh upon the wings of the wind:

Who maketh his angels spirits; his ministers a flaming fire:

Who laid the foundations of the earth, that it should not be removed for ever.

Thou coveredst it with the deep as with a garment; the waters stood above the mountains.

At thy rebuke they fled; at the voice of thy thunder they hasted away.

They go up by the mountains; they go down by the valleys unto the place which Thou hast founded for them.

Thou hast set a bound that they may not pass over; that they turn not again to cover the earth.

He sendeth the springs into the valleys, which run among the hills.

They give drink to every beast of the field: the wild asses quench their thirst.

By them shall the fowls of the heaven have their habitation, which sing among the branches.

He watereth the hills from his chambers: the earth is satisfied with the fruit of thy works.

He causeth the grass to grow for the cattle, and herb for the service of man: that he may bring forth food out of the earth;

And wine that maketh glad the heart of man, and

oil to make his face to shine, and bread which strengtheneth man's heart.

The trees of the Lord are full of sap; the cedars of Lebanon, which He hath planted;

Where the birds make their nests: as for the stork, the fir trees are her house.

The high hills are a refuge for the wild goats; and the rocks for the conies.

He appointed the moon for seasons: the sun knoweth his going down.

Thou makest darkness, and it is night: wherein all the beasts of the forest do creep forth.

The young lions roar after their prey, and seek their meat from God.

The sun ariseth, they gather themselves together, and lay them down in their dens.

Man goeth forth unto his work and to his labour until the evening.

O Lord, how manifold are thy works! in wisdom hast Thou made them all: the earth is full of thy riches.

So is this great and wide sea, wherein are things creeping innumerable, both small and great beasts.

There go the ships: there is that leviathan, whom Thou hast made to play therein.

These wait all upon Thee; that Thou mayest give them their meat in due season.

That Thou givest them they gather: Thou openest thine hand, they are filled with good.

Thou hidest thy face, they are troubled: Thou

takest away their breath, they die, and return to their dust.

Thou sendest forth thy spirit, they are created: and Thou renewest the face of the earth.

The glory of the Lord shall endure for ever: the Lord shall rejoice in his works.

He looketh on the earth, and it trembleth: He toucheth the hills, and they smoke.

I will sing unto the Lord as long as I live: I will sing praise to my God while I have my being.

My meditation of Him shall be sweet: I will be glad in the Lord.

Let the sinners be consumed out of the earth, and let the wicked be no more. Bless thou the Lord, O my soul. Praise ye the Lord.

—Psalm 104.

GREAT ART THOU, O LORD, and greatly to be praised; great is thy power, and thy wisdom infinite. Thou awakest us to delight in thy praise; for Thou madest us for thyself, and our heart is restless, until it repose in Thee. Grant me, Lord, to know and understand which is first, to call on Thee or to praise Thee? and, again, to know Thee or to call on Thee? For who can call on Thee, not knowing Thee? For he that knoweth Thee not, may call on Thee as other than Thou art. Or, is it rather, that we call on Thee that we may know Thee? But how shall they call on Him in whom they have not believed? or how shall they believe without a preacher? And they that seek the Lord shall praise Him. For they that seek shall find Him, and they that find shall praise Him.

—*The Confessions of St. Augustine.*

ADORATION PSALMS

A Hymn of God's Mercy in Forgiveness of Sins

Bless the Lord, O my soul: and all that is within me, bless his holy name.

Bless the Lord, O my soul, and forget not all his benefits:

Who forgiveth all thine iniquities; who healeth all thy diseases;

Who redeemeth thy life from destruction; who crowneth thee with lovingkindness and tender mercies;

Who satisfieth thy mouth with good things; so that thy youth is renewed like the eagle's.

The Lord executeth righteousness and judgment for all that are oppressed.

He made known his ways unto Moses, his acts unto the children of Israel.

The Lord is merciful and gracious, slow to anger, and plenteous in mercy.

He will not always chide: neither will He keep his anger for ever.

He hath not dealt with us after our sins; nor rewarded us according to our iniquities.

For as the heaven is high above the earth, so great is his mercy toward them that fear Him.

As far as the east is from the west, so far hath He removed our transgressions from us.

Like as a father pitieth his children, so the Lord pitieth them that fear Him.

For He knoweth our frame; He remembereth that we are dust.

As for man, his days are as grass: as a flower of the field, so he flourisheth.

For the wind passeth over it, and it is gone; and the place thereof shall know it no more.

But the mercy of the Lord is from everlasting to everlasting upon them that fear Him, and his righteousness unto children's children;

To such as keep his covenant, and to those that remember his commandments to do them.

The Lord hath prepared his throne in the heavens; and his kingdom ruleth over all.

Bless the Lord, ye his angels, that excel in strength, that do his commandments, hearkening unto the voice of his word.

Bless ye the Lord, all ye his hosts; ye ministers of his, that do his pleasure.

Bless the Lord, all his works in all places of his dominion: bless the Lord, O my soul.

—Psalm 103.

A Votive Anthem on the Work and Attributes of God

Praise ye the Lord. I will praise the Lord with my whole heart, in the assembly of the upright, and in the congregation.

ADORATION PSALMS

The works of the Lord are great, sought out of all them that have pleasure therein.

His work is honourable and glorious: and his righteousness endureth for ever.

He hath made his wonderful works to be remembered: the Lord is gracious and full of compassion.

He hath given meat unto them that fear Him: He will ever be mindful of his covenant.

He hath shewed his people the power of his works, that He may give them the heritage of the heathen.

The works of his hands are verity and judgment; all his commandments are sure.

They stand fast for ever and ever, and are done in truth and uprightness.

He sent redemption unto his people: He hath commanded his covenant for ever: holy and reverend is his name.

The fear of the Lord is the beginning of wisdom: a good understanding have all they that do his commandments; his praise endureth for ever.

—Psalm 111.

A Festal Anthem on God's Universal Rule

I will extol Thee, my God, O King; and I will bless thy name for ever and ever.

Every day will I bless Thee; and I will praise thy name for ever and ever.

Great is the Lord, and greatly to be praised; and his greatness is unsearchable.

One generation shall praise thy works to another, and shall declare thy mighty acts.

I will speak of the glorious honour of thy majesty, and of thy wondrous works.

And men shall speak of the might of thy terrible acts: and I will declare thy greatness.

They shall abundantly utter the memory of thy great goodness, and shall sing of thy righteousness.

The Lord is gracious, and full of compassion; slow to anger, and of great mercy.

The Lord is good to all: and his tender mercies are over all his works.

All thy works shall praise Thee, O Lord; and thy saints shall bless Thee.

They shall speak of the glory of thy kingdom, and talk of thy power;

To make known to the sons of men his mighty acts, and the glorious majesty of his Kingdom.

Thy Kingdom is an everlasting Kingdom, and thy dominion endureth throughout all generations.

The Lord upholdeth all that fall, and raiseth up all those that be bowed down.

The eyes of all wait upon Thee; and Thou givest them their meat in due season.

Thou openest thine hand, and satisfiest the desire of every living thing.

The Lord is righteous in all his ways, and holy in all his works.

The Lord is nigh unto all them that call upon Him, to all that call upon Him in truth.

ADORATION PSALMS

He will fulfil the desire of them that fear Him: He also will hear their cry, and will save them.

The Lord preserveth all them that love Him: but all the wicked will He destroy.

My mouth shall speak the praise of the Lord: and let all flesh bless his holy name for ever and ever.

—Psalm 145.

A Festal Anthem on Trust in God

Praise ye the Lord.   Praise the Lord, O my soul.

While I live will I praise the Lord: I will sing praises unto my God while I have any being.

Put not your trust in princes, nor in the son of man, in whom there is no help.

His breath goeth forth, he returneth to his earth; in that very day his thoughts perish.

Happy is he that hath the God of Jacob for his help, whose hope is in the Lord his God:

Which made heaven, and earth, the sea, and all that therein is: which keepeth truth for ever:

Which executeth judgment for the oppressed: which giveth food to the hungry.   The Lord looseth the prisoners:

The Lord openeth the eyes of the blind: the Lord raiseth them that are bowed down: the Lord loveth the righteous:

The Lord preserveth the strangers; He relieveth the fatherless and widow: but the way of the wicked He turneth upside down.

SELECTED PSALMS

The Lord shall reign for ever, even thy God, O Zion, unto all generations. Praise ye the Lord.

—Psalm 146.

A Festal Anthem on God's Rule in Nature and Mankind

Praise ye the Lord: for it is good to sing praises unto our God; for it is pleasant; and praise is comely.

The Lord doth build up Jerusalem; He gathereth together the outcasts of Israel.

He healeth the broken in heart, and bindeth up their wounds.

He telleth the number of the stars; He calleth them all by their names.

Great is our Lord, and of great power: his understanding is infinite.

The Lord lifteth up the meek: He casteth the wicked down to the ground.

Sing unto the Lord with thanksgiving; sing praise upon the harp unto our God:

Who covereth the heaven with clouds, who prepareth rain for the earth, who maketh grass to grow upon the mountains.

He giveth to the beast his food, and to the young ravens which cry.

He delighteth not in the strength of the horse: He taketh not pleasure in the legs of a man.

The Lord taketh pleasure in them that fear Him, in those that hope in his mercy.

ADORATION PSALMS

Praise the Lord, O Jerusalem; praise thy God, O Zion.

For He hath strengthened the bars of thy gates; He hath blessed thy children within thee.

He maketh peace in thy borders, and filleth thee with the finest of the wheat.

He sendeth forth his commandment upon earth: his word runneth very swiftly.

He giveth snow like wool: He scattereth the hoar frost like ashes.

He casteth forth his ice like morsels: who can stand before his cold?

He sendeth out his word, and melteth them: He causeth his wind to blow, and the waters flow.

He sheweth his word unto Jacob, his statutes and his judgments unto Israel.

He hath not dealt so with any nation: and as for his judgments, they have not known them.   Praise ye the Lord.

—Psalm 147.

---

*A Festal Anthem on Praise to God in Heaven
and on Earth*

Praise ye the Lord.   Praise ye the Lord from the heavens: praise Him in the heights.

Praise ye Him, all his angels: praise ye Him, all his hosts.

Praise ye Him, sun and moon: praise Him, all ye stars of light.

Praise Him, ye heavens of heavens, and ye waters that be above the heavens.

Let them praise the name of the Lord: for He commanded, and they were created.

He hath also stablished them for ever and ever: He hath made a decree which shall not pass.

Praise the Lord from the earth, ye dragons, and all deeps:

Fire, and hail; snow, and vapour; stormy wind fulfilling his word:

Mountains, and all hills; fruitful trees, and all cedars:

Beasts, and all cattle; creeping things, and flying fowl:

Kings of the earth, and all people; princes, and all judges of the earth:

Both young men, and maidens; old men, and children:

Let them praise the name of the Lord: for his name alone is excellent; his glory is above the earth and heaven.

He also exalteth the horn of his people, the praise of all his saints; even of the children of Israel, a people near unto Him.   Praise ye the Lord.

—Psalm 148.

" *The Doxology of the Psalter* " [1]

Praise ye the Lord.   Praise God in his sanctuary: praise Him in the firmament of his power.

[1] J. J. S. Perowne.   *The Book of Psalms* (Draper).

ADORATION PSALMS

Praise Him for his mighty acts: praise Him according to his excellent greatness.

Praise Him with the sound of the trumpet: praise Him with the psaltery and harp.

Praise Him with the timbrel and dance: praise Him with stringed instruments and organs.

Praise Him upon the loud cymbals: praise Him upon the high sounding cymbals.

Let every thing that hath breath praise the Lord. Praise ye the Lord.

—Psalm 150.

Not WHAT, but whom, I do believe,
        That, in my darkest hour of need,
Hath comfort that no mortal creed
        To mortal man may give;—
Not what, but whom!
        For Christ is more than all the creeds,
        And his full life of gentle deeds
        Shall all the creeds outlive.
Not what I do believe, but whom!
        Who walks beside me in the gloom?
        Who shares the burden wearisome.
        Who all the dim way doth illume,
        And bids me look beyond the tomb
        The larger life to live?—
Not what I do believe,
But whom!
Not what,
But whom!
    —JOHN OXENHAM *(Credo—Methuen, London).*

XIX

THE PRAYER OF JESUS

THESE things spake Jesus; and lifting up his
eyes to heaven, He said, Father, the hour is come;
glorify thy Son, that the Son may glorify Thee:
even as Thou gavest Him authority over all flesh,
that to all whom Thou hast given Him, He should
give eternal life. And this is life eternal, that they
should know Thee the only true God, and Him
whom Thou didst send, *even* Jesus Christ. I glorified Thee on the earth, having accomplished the
work which Thou hast given me to do. And now,
Father, glorify Thou Me with thine own self with
the glory which I had with Thee before the world
was. I manifested thy name unto the men whom
Thou gavest Me out of the world: thine they were,
and Thou gavest them to Me; and they have kept
thy word. Now they know that all things whatsoever Thou hast given Me are from Thee: for the
words which Thou gavest Me I have given unto
them; and they received *them,* and knew of a truth
that I came forth from Thee, and they believed that
Thou didst send Me. I pray for them: I pray not
for the world, but for those whom Thou hast given
Me; for they are thine: and all things that are
mine are thine, and thine are mine: and I am
glorified in them. And I am no more in the world,

and these are in the world, and I come to Thee.
Holy Father, keep them in thy name which Thou
hast given Me, that they may be one, even as We
are. While I was with them, I kept them in thy
name which Thou hast given Me: and I guarded
them, and not one of them perished, but the son of
perdition; that the Scripture might be fulfilled.
But now I come to Thee; and these things I speak
in the world, that they may have my joy made
full in themselves. I have given them thy word;
and the world hated them, because they are not of
the world, even as I am not of the world. I pray
not that Thou shouldest take them from the world,
but that Thou shouldest keep them from the evil
one. They are not of the world, even as I am not
of the world. Sanctify them in the truth: thy
word is truth. As Thou didst send Me into the
world, even so sent I them into the world. And
for their sakes I sanctify myself, that they themselves also may be sanctified in truth. Neither for
these only do I pray, but for them also that believe
on Me through their word; that they may all be
one; even as Thou, Father, *art* in Me, and I in
Thee, that they also may be in Us: that the world
may believe that Thou didst send Me. And the
glory which Thou hast given Me I have given unto
them; that they may be one, even as We *are* one;
I in them, and Thou in Me, that they may be per-
fected into one; that the world may know that Thou
didst send Me, and lovedst them, even as Thou

THE PRAYER OF JESUS

lovedst Me. Father, I desire that they also whom
Thou hast given Me be with Me where I am, that
they may behold my glory, which Thou hast given
Me: for Thou lovedst Me before the foundation of
the world. O righteous Father, the world knew
Thee not, but I knew Thee; and these knew that
Thou didst send Me; and I made known unto them
thy name, and will make it known; that the love
wherewith Thou lovedst Me may be in them, and
I in them.

—JOHN 17 (R. V.).

XX

DOES GOD SPEAK?

It was the Gray Dawn of time when—
Man first caught within himself the living light,
And, henceforth, muffled voices within us have been the
    echoes of God.
For He is the Living Voice.

It was Sunrise to me when—
He awakened me, saying: "Ask of Me, and I will give
    thee the nations for thine inheritance,
And the uttermost parts of the earth for thy possession."
Then, spilling sunlight through the distant years, He called
    me to the vision of his triumph.
For He is the Living Revealer.

It was Noon to me when—
In the sanctuary of prayer I set forth my claim to kinship
    with God and the spiritual value of the fellowship of
    souls,
And, forthwith, a warm, living light flashed through me like
    a great shooting star.
For He is the Living Hope.

It was the Sunset of the world when—
Beside the sacrificial altar I beheld that I am an heir of
    the universe with its crowns of living gold,
And, from beneath the shadow of the Cross, a radiant
    light poured out on the pathway to the Throne.
For He is the Living Redeemer.

XXI

THE LORD'S PRAYER

AND HE said unto them, When ye pray say: Our Father who are in heaven, Hallowed be thy name. Thy Kingdom come. Thy will be done on earth, as it is in heaven. Give us this day our daily bread. And forgive us our trespasses, as we forgive those who trespass against us. And lead us not into temptation; but deliver us from evil: for thine is the Kingdom, and the power, and the glory, for ever and ever. Amen.

www.ingramcontent.com/pod-product-compliance
Lightning Source LLC
Chambersburg PA
CBHW051824040426
42447CB00006B/352